WE SPEAK

OVER

WE SPEAK FROM THE AIR
and
OVER TO YOU

Broadcasts by the R.A.F.

Originally issued for the Air Ministry by the Ministry of Information, 1942 and 1943

A Goodall paperback
from
Crécy Publishing Limited

ISBN 9 780907 579939

FSC
MIX
Paper
FSC® C110322

Printed in Malta
by Melita Press

A Goodall paperback
published by

Crécy Publishing Limited
1a Ringway Trading Estate, Shadowmoss Road, Manchester M22 5LH
Tel: 0161 499 0024   Fax: 0161 499 0298
www.crecy.co.uk

PUBLISHER'S NOTE

During the Second World War nearly 1,200 radio broadcasts were made by serving RAF personnel, describing their operational and combat experiences 'in their own words'. As real-time eye-witness accounts of the battles and daily business of war, these broadcasts became immensely popular with an audience hungry for real news from the front line. Subsequently, more than fifty transcripts of the broadcasts were printed in two books, *We Speak from the Air* and *Over to You*, published by the Ministry of Information on behalf of the Air Ministry in 1942 and 1943. These two volumes are now brought together in a single book for the first time.

When these accounts were broadcast, the war was still raging and the nation was, in every respect, fighting for survival. Nevertheless, the accounts were written with a tone of understatement and coolness, a matter-of-factness about a job that had to be done and was worth doing, an embodiment of the wartime spirit. The authors were also, of course, coldly dismissive of 'the Hun'.

These books were not only intended to reassure the public that 'our lads', and their many overseas colleagues, were on the winning side, but also to encourage fellow service men and women; a note in the originals states 'There are many men and women in the Forces who would welcome a chance to read this book. If you hand it in at any post office, it will go to them.'

Published in 1942, the first volume, *We Speak from the Air*, describes operations over land and sea, over Britain and the Continent, and the extracts provide 'the human stories behind the official communiqués, and show us the great range and effectiveness of our Air Power'. The companion volume, *Over to You*, appeared the following year and is able to look back on 'the legendary days of Dunkirk and the Battle of Britain [and] the winged victory in North Africa', as well as the work of Ferry Command and pilot training in Canada.

The two volumes together provide a wealth of fascinating eyewitness accounts of wartime combat, recorded at the time by those actually involved in the day-to-day business of war. Those who related their experiences did not all survive to see the victory that would eventually be achieved, but their words and deeds live on.

WE SPEAK FROM THE AIR

Men of the R.A.F. describe their own experiences in their own words. These accounts of operations over Germany, France, Holland, Belgium, Britain, Norway, Italy, the North Sea, the English Channel and the Atlantic give us the human stories behind the official communiqués, and show us the great range and effectiveness of our Air Power. The narratives are selected from over 280 broadcasts, given anonymously by the R.A.F. and W.A.A.F. during 1941.

WE SPEAK FROM THE AIR

Speak for the air, your element, your hunters

Who range across the ribbed and shifting sky:

Speak for whatever gives you mastery –

Wings that bear out your purpose, quick-responsive

Fingers, a fighting heart, a kestrel's eye.

Speak of the rough and tumble in the blue,

The mast-high run, the flak, the battering gales:

You that, until the life you love prevails,

Must follow Death's impersonal vocation –

Speak from the air and tell your hunters' tales.

CONTENTS

1. AIRCRAFT CAPTURES U-BOAT

HUDSON AIRCRAFT OF COASTAL COMMAND RECENTLY
SIGHTED AND ATTACKED A U-BOAT IN THE ATLANTIC.
AS A RESULT OF THIS ATTACK THE U-BOAT WAS FORCED
TO THE SURFACE IN A BADLY DAMAGED CONDITION
AND SURRENDERED. (Admiralty and Air Ministry Communiqué)

We knew early in the morning that there was a U-boat somewhere round that part of the Atlantic. Another Hudson out on patrol from my squadron had seen her twice, but both times she dived and got away.

The Atlantic didn't look very inviting when we left that morning. The sea was rough, and covered with angry white-caps. The clouds were low, and we kept on running into rain-storms and patches of dirty weather. We flew a good many miles close down to the sea – nothing to look at but clouds, and waves, and rain, and it was getting a bit monotonous. The first thing I knew about the U-boat was a shout from my second pilot, 'There's one just in front of you.' He pointed out to the port bow, and there was a U-boat, roughly 1,200 yards away, just starting to crash-dive – they had seen us too.

The second pilot was standing with his face pressed to the windscreen, and he had a better view than I had, so I called out to him, 'Let me know when it's time to attack, Jack.' He nodded, and a few seconds later my whole crew shouted, 'Now!'

When I came round again in a tight turn, the whole area of the sea was churned up into a foaming mass, and in the middle of it the U-boat suddenly popped to the surface again. So we dived straight on to her and opened up with all the guns we had. I had my front guns going, the wireless operator dropped on his tummy and wound down the belly gun in the floor of the aircraft, and the gunner in the turret was firing practically the whole time. We had tracer ammunition loaded, and the red streaks of the tracer were flashing all round the conning-tower, and showering up the water all round the hull of the U-boat.

To our surprise, just as we dived in again to the attack, the conning-tower hatch was flung open, and about a dozen men tumbled out, and slid down on to the deck. We thought at first they were making for their guns, so we kept our own guns going hard. The Germans who had already got out of the conning-tower didn't like that a bit, and they tried to scramble back again. The rest of the crew were still trying to get out of the hatch, and they sort of met in the middle and argued it out. It was a regular shambles for a few minutes. We could see them very clearly, for we were close on top of them, and they were wearing bright yellow life-saving jackets, rather like our Mae Wests.

11

While the Germans were all stooging about in the conning-tower we continued to attack them, circling round each time and coming in again. That made the confusion below even worse.

We went round four times, and we were just getting ready to dive on them for the fifth time when they decided they had had enough of it. They stuck a white rag of some sort out of the conning-tower, and waved it violently. We found out afterwards that it was a shirt they were using for a white flag.

We all stopped firing, but continued to circle them with all our guns trained. The Germans were determined to make us understand that they had surrendered. They got hold of some sort of white board, and waved that at us too.

We were still suspicious, so I dived right over the U-boat at about 50 feet, and then flew alongside her, to see what it was all about. They followed us all round with their white flag. We followed them all round with our guns trained on them.

Practically the whole crew seemed to be in the conning-tower now, packed in so tightly they could hardly move. We were close enough to see their faces, and a glummer-looking lot I never saw in my life. Not a smile among them!

It was only then that we began to realise that we really had captured a submarine, and they really had surrendered. The difficulty then was how to get them in. I even suggested jokingly that I should drop my second pilot by parachute as prize crew, but he didn't fancy it. But we were determined to get them ashore if we could, submarine and all, so we sent off signals to our base, asking for surface craft to be sent to pick them up. We soon knew that several were on their way, steaming as hard as they could go, and other aircraft were being diverted to relieve us.

All we had to do was to keep circling the U-boat with our guns trained, to prevent the crew going below; we had to intimidate the crew, and keep them in the conning-tower. We kept that up for three and a half hours, and it was a bit trying. I dared not take my eyes off them for a single second – and when we finished circling at last, I couldn't turn my head at all, my neck was so stiff. The wireless operator had even a worse job. He spent his three and a half hours signalling furiously.

At last a relief aircraft turned up, a Coastal Command Catalina flying boat. We saw it coming, and we were scared it was going to attack the U-boat, so we flew towards it signalling hard that she had surrendered, and we were trying to take her prisoner. I think the actual signal we flashed was: 'Look after *our* sub., it has shown the white flag.'

The Catalina boys understood, and they started to circle her too. Then another Hudson came up, and plenty more aircraft as the day wore on, but our petrol was getting a bit short, so we had to turn for home, and that was the last we saw of our U-boat.

Of course the job wasn't anything like finished. We had had the incredible good luck to find the U-boat, but the Catalinas kept up the watch for hours, much longer than we did, through gales and darkness. They stuck on to the U-boat magnificently. Then the Navy came along, and they put up a grand show too, taking the U-boat in tow in the most difficult conditions, and bringing her right in to shore, with all the crew prisoners.

And we owe the Navy a personal word of thanks, too, for a very nice gesture they made. They came down to our station and handed over to the squadron a rather wonderful memento of the occasion, a memento of which we shall always be very proud – the U-boat's flag.

2. MAST-HIGH OVER ROTTERDAM

A HIGHLY SUCCESSFUL DAYLIGHT RAID WAS CARRIED
OUT THIS AFTERNOON ON ENEMY SHIPPING IN THE
DOCKS AT ROTTERDAM. SEVERAL SQUADRONS OF
BLENHEIMS OF BOMBER COMMAND WERE ENGAGED
IN THE OPERATION AND THE ATTACK WAS PRESSED
HOME WITH GREAT DARING FROM VERY LOW LEVELS.
(Air Ministry Communiqué)

The first I saw of Rotterdam was a sky-line of high cranes over the docks. Climbing as high as the cranes themselves were fat columns of black smoke to mark the shipping that had already been successfully bombed. I was in the second formation of Blenheims to attack.

I had watched the leading squadron cross the Dutch coast only a few feet above the sandy beaches, where people waved us on, and I wondered if they had noticed the R.A.F. unconsciously giving the 'V' for Victory sign as we flew over in vic formation. There was the astonishing flatness that I had expected and only occasionally could I feel the aircraft lifted up to miss windmills, farmhouses and villages; but most of all I was delighted to see that the country Dutchmen really do wear baggy trousers and vivid blue shirts. Cows galloped nervously about as we came hedge-hopping over the fields. Nearly everyone we saw gave us some kind of cheery gesture: but one man, evidently alarmed, was crouching against a telegraph pole. Actually we were so low that a few of my friends brought back some evidence of it. One pilot, for instance, not only cut straight through a crane cable, but got a dent in the belly of his aircraft, and some red dust, scraped from a Dutch chimney-pot, stuck to his aircraft. The same pilot had evidently been corn-cutting in between the hedges and returned with a small sheaf of the stuff in a niche on the leading edge of his wing.

We bombed Rotterdam at 4.55 in the afternoon. As we flashed across the docks, the observer saw 'our' ship – a bulky black hull and one funnel. We nipped across the last building and from mast-height we let our load drop. She was a medium-sized ship – I should guess about 4,000 tons. I could feel the bomb doors springing to, and then we were away over towards the town. In ship bombing of this kind, often you can't see your results; but I had a very clear view of our own results this time. There was a terrific explosion and instantaneous smoke and flames. I have seen lots of these explosions by now, but this one was by far the biggest. Over to the left we saw a good many supply vessels burning from the attack by the first wave. Elsewhere burning warehouses obstructed the view and only the bombers following on could see what had happened.

And then on our way out of the town, with white tracers whipping under us, I saw great pillars of smoke spring up from the other enemy ships we had bombed.

We had a good trip home and it had been a great day.

3. FIGHTER PILOT

THE KING HAS BEEN GRACIOUSLY PLEASED TO
APPROVE THE FOLLOWING AWARDS, IN RECOGNITION
OF GALLANTRY DISPLAYED IN FLYING OPERATIONS
AGAINST THE ENEMY:
SECOND BAR TO THE DISTINGUISHED FLYING CROSS.
ACTING SQUADRON LEADER — THIS OFFICER HAS
DISPLAYED A CONSPICUOUS GALLANTRY AND
INITIATIVE IN SEARCHING FOR AND ATTACKING
ENEMY RAIDERS, OFTEN IN ADVERSE WEATHER
CONDITIONS. SINCE DECEMBER, 1940, HE HAS
DESTROYED THREE ENEMY BOMBERS AND ONE
FIGHTER, THUS BRINGING HIS TOTAL VICTORIES TO
TWENTY-TWO. (Air Ministry Bulletin)

When war broke out, I had been in the R.A.F. some four years and was
delighted when I was posted as a flight commander to a new Spitfire
squadron which had just been formed. We put in some pretty intensive
training, and long before the spring of 1940 arrived we were right up to the
mark and ready to go.

Our first combat chanced to be with a large formation of Me. 109's,
Nazi single-seater fighters. It took place over the coast of North Belgium,
and the first thing I noticed after we had closed with them was that the air
seemed to be full of planes milling around. I singled one out and was lucky
enough to shoot him down in a wood near St. Omer. On that first meeting
the squadron shot down eleven Huns for the loss of one of our pilots, who
had crash-landed on the beach.

That wood near St. Omer will be one of the first places I shall visit
when we have won the war, because while out on our second patrol that
same afternoon I shot down two Me. 110's right alongside it. I had picked
the first one out of a large party covering a bunch of Ju. 87's which were
dive-bombing the harbour, and I forced him to crash-land alongside the
wreckage of my morning Me. 109.

Incidentally the pilot of that Me. 110 very nearly put an early end to my
fighting career with nothing more than a pistol. I had circled him very low
to make sure he had crashed, when he stepped out of the cockpit
apparently unhurt and took a pot-shot at me with his pistol. It was either
wizard shooting or the world's biggest fluke, for that shot went through my
windscreen within an inch or two of my head. I turned quickly and dealt
with him, and as I did so I saw that another 110 had been snooping along
behind me over the tree-tops, hoping to pick me off. He opened up with

cannon fire and put a shell through my fuselage, but I did a tight turn, squirted at him with what ammunition I had left, and he went down to crash alongside his two friends.

As you can imagine, I was pretty bucked with that bag of three for my first day in action, and a couple of Dornier 17's the next day and another of the same type on the third day made me quite a lot happier. The second three were bagged over the Dunkirk-Calais-Boulogne area, and the last affair was a regular shooting match. I remember I arrived back at my base with no oil, no glycol, and the sliding hood and side door of my Spitfire shot away. I had a cannon shot through the tail which left only two inches play on the elevators with which to land, and I had no flaps, no brakes and a flat tyre. I did somehow manage to put it down all right, and as I finished my landing run the engine seized up. That Spitfire was too shot up and damaged to fly again, but I was lucky enough to escape with only a slight wound in the thigh, caused by a bit of metal flying off the rudder bar.

I was fit again within a few days and, early on the morning of the first day I was back, nine of us came upon a bunch of Heinkel bombers with a high escort of about fifty Me. 109 fighters. I think pretty well all of us had picked off one of the Hun bombers each before down came the fighters. A few minutes later we had to try and make our way home because both petrol and ammunition were getting short. I was in a bit of a spot by then with six Me. 109's after me, but luckily I found a nice big friendly cloud in which I was able to turn and shoot down one of my pursuers into the sea with what ammunition I had left. Then I popped back into the cloud and arrived home with only five gallons of petrol left and five shell holes in my Spitfire. 'All the boys home safely' was the entry in my log after that little affair.

When the hectic Dunkirk days had ended, the squadron was sent into a quiet sector to rest and reorganise, and I remember a particularly enjoyable incident which happened one morning around the middle of August. Up at 15,000 feet over Cardiff I had picked up three Ju. 88's which were heading as if for Ireland. My stern attacks didn't seem to make the slightest impression on them, so I hared past them, turned and carried out head-on attacks. That worked all right, but by the time I had accounted for two of them the third had disappeared in the clouds.

A few days later, when I was on my way to an aerodrome to get some of the holes in my Spitfire patched up, I struck the first of the big daylight blitzes on the South Coast, and ran into a couple of Ju. 88's off Beachy Head. I chased one of them about thirty-five miles out to sea before I shot him down. By that time we were right down on the water and as I turned and climbed the other Hun opened fire at me with his cannon. He shot my oil and glycol tanks away and part of my propeller, which caused excessive vibration. I climbed for all I was worth and pushed the engine flat out. Very soon it was on fire but, even so, it got me back sixty miles before it went up in smoke and I had to bale out. I was smothered in oil and couldn't see a thing. Perhaps it was just as well, for if I'd realised I was only a few hundred feet up I'd probably never have had the nerve to jump. As it was, my 'chute opened with a bump a second or so before my feet hit the earth. Some Observer Corps men I spoke to later told me I was not more than 500 feet up when I jumped. I still go hot and cold when I think of that jump.

Incidentally I gained an Iron Cross that evening. In the base hospital to which I was taken with an injured leg, I was put in a bed next to a German pilot who had been badly burned. He couldn't sleep and he could speak English perfectly – he told me he had spent his honeymoon in this country – I lay awake talking to him. He insisted on giving me his Iron Cross, which I always carry with me now as a mascot.

It was after I had returned from this spell of sick leave that I had an experience which made me angrier than anything I can remember for a long time. I was shot down by a lone bomber – a most undignified experience for a fighter pilot. It was a Dornier and I ran into him as he was bombing shipping about fifteen miles off the south coast of Wales. I shot him down all right, but as he went seawards his rear gunner got in a burst which put two holes in my cylinders, and I just managed to scrape in on to the very edge of the cliffs near Tenby. I was knocked out in the crash, but fortunately not for long, and I leapt out of that cockpit pretty quickly when I heard the petrol sizzling on the hot engine!

September 11th of last year is a day I shall always remember, for it was then I was promoted and given command of the Burma Squadron of Hurricanes. The first day I took them into action was a Sunday four days after my arrival. We found a big bunch of mixed bombers, flying in formations of anything from thirty to sixty, with escorting fighters above them. As I led my new squadron in, I saw three of these parties nearing London. As the boys waded into the bombers, I went for some of the fighters. I picked off an Me. 110 which I shot down over Barking, and one of his pals nearly got his own back when he put a bullet through my windscreen a few inches from my head. The squadron had a bag of five in that first outing, and there was quite a party in the Mess that night.

It was soon after this show that I had one of the luckiest breaks on record. I had been ordered up in rather bad cloud and hadn't been in the air ten minutes when I was told by radio that an enemy aircraft was near me. I hadn't finished acknowledging the information when I came out of the cloud, and there, dead in my sights and not 100 yards away, a Ju. 88 was waffling contentedly along. I yelled into my telephone, 'Good heavens, he's here,' pressed my gun-button as I spoke, and the raider crashed near Southwold.

4. FORTRESS RAIDER

SEVERAL OTHER ATTACKS WERE MADE IN THE
COURSE OF THE AFTERNOON. A FORTRESS AIRCRAFT
REACHED EMDEN, AND FOUND FINE WEATHER OVER
THE TARGET. BOMBS WERE SEEN TO BURST IN THE
TARGET AREA, AND SMOKE CURLED UP FROM THE
GROUND FAR BELOW. (Air Ministry Bulletin)

I have flown in the sub-stratosphere in a Fortress bomber over Holland, France, Norway and Germany. If the people on the ground in those countries have seen us at all, we have appeared no more than the tiniest dot in the sky. Their largest towns to us have seemed no bigger than a sardine tin laid flat on the perspex.

On your first ascent, you are very much aware of flying in unexplored space, relying completely on oxygen, but after a few trips you become accustomed to new colours in the sky; and when from one point, only a hundred miles from the English coast, you can see right across Denmark into the Baltic, and into Germany by Hamburg, and the whole plain of Holland is spread out in front of you, you do little more than note it in your log. To us who have carried out a good many attacks on the enemy, our Fortress seems no more difficult or less reliable than a good old Lysander at 1,000 feet. It's all a question of what you get used to.

Before coming to our attack on Emden last week-end, I should like to give you two instances of why we have learned to have this trust in the Fortresses. I was in the Fortress which was attacked by seven fighters when we were returning from Brest. Three minutes after our bombs had gone, the fire controller called out that there were seven enemy fighters coming up to us from the starboard quarter, 1,000 feet below. They closed in and there was almost no part of the Fortress which was not hit. Some of my friends in the crew were killed, others wounded. A petrol tank was punctured, bomb doors were thrown open, flaps were put out of action, tail tab shot away, tail wheel stuck half down, brakes not working, only one aileron any good and the rudder almost out of control. The centre of the fuselage had become a tangle of wires and broken cables, square feet of the wings had been shot away, and still the pilot managed to land the Fortress on a strange aerodrome. There is a testimony to the makers in America. Another time, when we were coming away from Oslo, part of the oxygen supply ceased and the pilot had to dive down swiftly through 19,000 feet. He pulled out and the Fortress landed safely at base. There is proof of the strength of the Fortress's construction.

Fortunately these thrills are rare. Our attack on Emden last week-end was almost without incident, except, of course, for the dropping of the bombs by the Sperry sight with beautiful accuracy on the target. It was, in fact, a typical Fortress raid. We lost sight of the aerodrome at 2,000 feet, and never saw ground again until we were off the Dutch islands. Foamy white cloud, like the froth on a huge tankard of beer, stretched all over England and for about thirty miles out to sea. The horizon turned – quite suddenly – from purple to green and from green to yellow. There was a haze over Germany, but I could see Emden fifty miles away. I called out to the pilot, in the sort of jargon that we use in the air, 'Stand by for bombing, bomb-sight in detent, George in, O.K., I've got her.' Then the pilot says to me, 'Let her go.'

The drill is that I push a lever on my left for the bomb doors to open, and on a dial in my cabin two arms move out like the hands of a clock to show me the position of the bomb doors. On and around the Sperry sight there are eleven knobs, two levers and two switches to operate. On the bombing panel there are five switches and three levers to work and the automatic camera to start. I keep my eye down the sighting tube which, incidentally, contains twenty-six prisms, and with my wrist I work the release. As the cross-hairs centred over a shining pin-point in Emden on which the sun was glinting, the bombs went down. The pilot was told by means of an automatic light which flickered on as they dropped. We were still two miles away from Emden when we turned away. One of the gunners watched the burst. Almost a minute later he told us through the inter-com., 'There you are, bursts in the centre of the something target,' and back we came through those extraordinary tints of the sky.

Over England there was a strange scene that I have noticed before. The cloud formation exactly compared with the land below. Every bay and inlet was repeated in the strata-cumulus thousands of feet above, like a white canopy over the island. During the whole sortie I had only one thrilling moment. I saw a Messerschmitt coming towards us. He seemed an improved type, and I looked again. It was a mosquito which had got stuck on the perspex in the take-off and had frozen stiff. The windows usually are splashed with insect blood, but this fellow had seemed the right shape for a Hun. Otherwise it was an uneventful, typical trip in a Fortress, with the temperature at minus 30 degrees below zero Centigrade.

5. BEAUFORT V. BATTLESHIP

SHORTLY BEFORE MIDNIGHT LAST NIGHT (THURSDAY)
A BLENHEIM AIRCRAFT OF COASTAL COMMAND ON
RECONNAISSANCE OFF THE SOUTHERN COAST OF
NORWAY SIGHTED AN ENEMY POCKET BATTLESHIP
ESCORTED BY A NUMBER OF DESTROYERS.
A STRIKING FORCE WAS DESPATCHED BY COASTAL
COMMAND AND IN THE EARLY HOURS OF THIS
MORNING THE BATTLESHIP, THEN OFF EGERSUND, WAS
HIT BY A TORPEDO FROM A BEAUFORT AIRCRAFT.
DENSE CLOUDS OF WHITE SMOKE ROSE FROM THE
VESSEL AND PREVENTED ACCURATE OBSERVATION BY
OTHER AIRCRAFT OF THE RESULTS OF THEIR ATTACKS.
(Air Ministry Communiqué)

Friday, June 13th was not a lucky day for the German Navy. A Coastal Command Beaufort aircraft, of which I was the pilot, obtained a direct hit with a torpedo on a German pocket battleship as it was slinking out past Norway, and sent it, with its attendant destroyers, back home.

When it was getting near midnight on Thursday we had orders to push off with other aircraft from the squadron. Somebody mentioned that it would soon be the 13th, and when my wireless operator found that we had to take pigeon container No. 13 he said, 'We're bound to be lucky.'

Carrying our torpedo slung beneath us, we started off in formation. There was a bit of moon, but it was partly obscured and shone through the haze only occasionally. In some patches of cloud you could see hardly anything, but it was fairly light in the clear spaces. We were well over the North Sea when midnight came. We were flying pretty high as we approached the coast of Southern Norway and found several gaps in the clouds where the moon was breaking through. You could see the surface of the water and, as we came into one of these clearings, we suddenly spotted a formation of enemy warships away down under the starboard wing. The white washes trailing behind them caught our eyes first, and then we saw the ships' small black slim shapes. They were arranged in a very nice formation with the pocket battleship in the middle and her five escorting destroyers dispersed around her. One destroyer was right ahead of the battleship and there were two more destroyers on each side, making a pretty effective screen. We dived to get into position from which to attack. We came down to a few hundred feet above the sea and flew at right angles across the stern of two destroyers bringing up at the rear. That put us on the broadside of the formation. We made a right-about turn to starboard and came straight back on its beam.

There was not much time to think about attacks. One destroyer was right in our way and I had to skid round its stern to get a suitable angle to drop. We were close enough to the destroyer to see the design of its camouflage, outlines of the deck fittings, and even the rail. The next second I put the nose of the aircraft round and saw the battleship in my sight. I pressed a button on the throttle which released the torpedo – and away it went.

As soon as the torpedo had gone I made a sharp turn to port and opened my engine flat out. I was expecting a barrage of flak at any moment. The navigator beside me was looking back at the ship saying, 'It's coming, it's coming.' But fortunately the flak did not come, not even when, for one unpleasant moment, we found ourselves in a vertical turn round one of the destroyers where we should have been easy meat. I think our attack must have taken them completely by surprise. All this time the torpedo was running on its course and really only a few seconds had elapsed.

As we flew clear from the ship, the rear gunner and the wireless operator shouted together over the inter-com., 'You've hit it. There's a great column of water going up, and dirty white smoke.'

I flew round in a circle to see for myself, and sure enough there was plenty of smoke and a patch of foam on the ship's track. Naturally I didn't want to hang around too long, so when we were satisfied with the results of our attack, we made a signal reporting it.

When we got back home we heard that other aircraft had found the German force after we had attacked it. The ships had stopped by then and were trying to hide themselves behind the smoke-screen made by the destroyer. Still later we learned that the formation had turned back to the Skagerrak and was limping home at reduced speed.

6. THE ATTACK ON AALESUND

THE HARBOUR AND ANCHORAGES OF THE
NORWEGIAN PORT OF AALESUND – ONE OF THE BASES
FROM WHICH HITLER SUPPLIES HIS NORTHERN
RUSSIAN FRONT – WERE WREATHED IN SMOKE AND
FLAMES FOR HOURS LAST NIGHT AND THIS MORNING
FOLLOWING THE MOST DEVASTATING SHIPPING
ATTACK EVER CARRIED OUT BY A SINGLE SQUADRON
OF THE R.A.F. (Air Ministry Bulletin)

It was still daylight when we set off over the North Sea, but darkness fell while we were on our way across. As we reached the Norwegian coast a bright moon was shining, which lit up the snow-covered mountains and countryside. We crossed an outer belt of small islands before coming to our target, which was shipping in the anchorage at Aalesund.

In the anchorage itself there were several medium-sized ships at anchor.

We were the second aircraft to arrive on the scene. The first arrival seemed to be drawing plenty of flak, while below him one of the ships was already burning furiously and dense clouds of smoke were drifting across the bay.

My crew and I decided it would be best to float round for a time in order to find the best target and then choose the right moment for our attack. So we circled the bay, watching the other Hudsons doing their stuff.

Several of them were attacking the ships from only a few feet above the sea, and it was most entertaining for us, at any rate, to watch the multi-coloured flak streaming downwards at them from the hills around. But the guns didn't seem to be having much luck, and the only targets I could see them hitting were the ships they were supposed to protect.

After one of these attacks I noticed a second ship starting to burn. Before long you could see a dull glow from its red-hot plates and then a mass of flames. At the same moment I saw a bomb burst alongside the large fish-oil factory in the harbour.

In the meanwhile my crew and I were so fascinated by all these interesting sights that we almost forgot about our own job. However, by now I had had plenty of opportunity of choosing my own particular target and to decide the best way to attack it.

I had selected the biggest ship of the lot, and as it was still afloat, I thought I'd have a shot at dive-bombing her from a good height – especially as the flak was now concentrating entirely on the low-flying aircraft.

So we climbed to about 6,000 feet and approached the target area from the sea. About five miles off Aalesund I throttled back, made a silent approach and, when we were almost directly over the ship, shoved my nose down, dropping a stick of heavy bombs right across her. The A. A. gunners must have been completely taken by surprise, as their guns didn't open up on us until we were well away.

Then I circled the ship again to have a look at results. At first we saw nothing unusual and thought we'd missed her. But suddenly our Canadian gunner shouted over the intercom., 'I think I can see a glow from right inside the ship,' and the next time we looked she was definitely down at the bows. A couple of minutes later the forecastle was well awash; then the water was up to her funnel and the rudder rose clear of the sea.

I shouted to my crew, 'Her boilers ought to burst any moment now,' and sure enough a minute or two later there was a violent explosion amidships. Dense clouds of steam shot up into the air and in a very short while all we could see above the water was the flag flying from her stern, and that very soon disappeared.

As we set course for home, fifteen minutes after we had dropped our bombs, all that remained were three boatloads of survivors rowing like hell for the shore.

7. SWEEPS OVER FRANCE

AN IRISH FLIGHT LIEUTENANT WHO WAS RECENTLY AWARDED A SECOND BAR TO HIS D.F.C. AND WHO LEADS A FLIGHT OF A FAMOUS AUSTRALIAN SQUADRON SHOT DOWN HIS 21ST ENEMY AIRCRAFT TO-DAY (THURSDAY), JUST A FEW DAYS BEFORE HIS 2IST BIRTHDAY. (Air Ministry Bulletin)

I've been on about fifty sweeps, and most of my victories have been gained over France. I've got my bag because I've been blessed with a pair of good eyes, and have learned to shoot straight. I've not been shot down – touch wood – and I've only once been badly shot up (I hope that doesn't sound Irish). And for all that I've got a lot to thank the pilots in my section. They are Australians and I've never met a more loyal or gamer crowd of chaps. They've saved my bacon many a time when I've been attacked from behind while concentrating on a Messerschmitt in front of me, and they've followed me through thick and thin. On the ground they're the cheeriest friends a fellow could have. I'm sure that Australia must be a grand country if it's anything like its pilots, and after the war I'm going to see it. No, not flying, or farming. I like a job with figures – accountancy or auditing.

Perhaps that doesn't sound much like a fighter pilot. But pilots are perfectly normal people.

Before going off on a trip I usually have a funny feeling in my tummy, but once I'm in my aircraft everything is fine. The brain is working fast, and if the enemy is met it seems to work like a clockwork motor. Accepting that, rejecting that, sizing up this, and remembering that. You don't have time to feel anything. But your nerves may be on edge – not from fear, but from excitement and the intensity of the mental effort.

I have come back from a sweep to find my shirt and tunic wet through with perspiration.

Our chaps sometimes find that they can't sleep. What happens is this. You come back from a show and find it very hard to remember what happened. Maybe you have a clear impression of three or four incidents, which stand out like illuminated lantern slides in the mind's eye. Perhaps a picture of two Me. 109's belting down on your tail from out of the sun and already within firing range. Perhaps another picture of your cannon shells striking at the belly of an Me. and the aircraft spraying debris around. But for the life of you, you can't remember what you did.

Later, when you have turned in and sleep is stealing over you, some tiny link in the forgotten chain of events comes back. Instantly you are fully awake, and then the whole story of the operation pieces itself together and you lie there, sleep driven away, re-living the combat, congratulating yourself for this thing, blaming yourself for that.

The reason for this is simply that everything happens so quickly in the air that you crowd a tremendous amount of thinking, action and emotion into a very short space of time, and you suffer afterwards from mental indigestion.

The other week I was feeling a little jaded. Then my seven days' leave came round, and I went back bursting with energy. On my first flight after getting back I shot down three Me.'s in one engagement, and the next day bagged two more. That shows the value of a little rest.

It's a grand life, and I know I'm lucky to be among the squadrons that are carrying out the sweeps.

The tactical side of the game is quite fascinating. You get to learn, for instance, how to fly so that all the time you have a view behind you as well as in front. The first necessity in combat is to see the other chap before he sees you, or at least before he gets the tactical advantage of you. The second is to hit him when you fire. You mightn't have a second chance.

After a dog-fight your section gets split up, and you must get together again, or tack on to others. The straggler is easy meat for a bunch of Jerries. Luckily, the chaps in my flight keep with me very well, and we owe a lot to it. On one occasion recently I saw an Me. dive on to one of my flight. As I went in after him, another Me. tailed in behind to attack me, but one of my flight went in after him. Soon half a dozen of us were flying at 400 m.p.h. in line astern, everybody, except the leader, firing at the chap in front of him.

I got my Hun just as my nearest pal got the Hun on my tail, and we were then three Spitfires in the lead. When we turned to face the other Me.'s we found that several others had joined in, but as we faced them they turned and fled.

The nearest I've been to being shot down was when another pilot and I attacked a Ju. 88. The bomber went down to sea level, so that we could only attack from above, in face of the fire of the Ju.'s rear guns. We put that Ju. into the sea all right, but I had to struggle home with my aircraft riddled with bullets and the undercarriage shot away.

I force-landed without the undercarriage, and was none the worse for it. But it wasn't very nice at the time.

Well, as I said just now, one day I'm planning to go to Australia – and audit books.

8. CONDOR WRITTEN OFF

A FOCKE-WULF CONDOR, ON THE WAY TO ATTACK
ATLANTIC CONVOYS, WAS INTERCEPTED TO-DAY BY A
LOCKHEED HUDSON OF THE R.A.F. COASTAL
COMMAND... (Air Ministry Bulletin)

The Focke-Wulf which we disposed of is by no means the first one to have been shot down in the Battle of the Atlantic. But this time it happens to have been written off by one of the Hudson squadrons which are now in action day and night over the wide battlefield of the Western Ocean.

My crew and I have been on the job of escorting and protecting convoys in the Atlantic for months past. It's largely monotonous work, helping to keep the shipping lanes safe – arduous and unspectacular work which has to be done mostly in wretched weather conditions so far as visibility is concerned.

It is work that doesn't often come into the news. It's a real case of no news being good news. While the convoys are going through safely without molestation from the air or from surface raiders and U-boats, there is no news. All is well. But my crew and I were longing for some liveliness. The other day we got a real packet of it.

It happened like this. Away out in the Atlantic, hours after dawn, we made our rendezvous with the convoy and the escorting warships. We did our usual stuff over them for more than a couple of hours, circling round and round in wide sweeps looking for possible danger. There wasn't a sign of anything in the air or on the sea. My relief was well on the way out and my fuel was getting a bit low, so I signalled 'Good-bye and good luck' to the convoy.

I was just setting course for home when something – I don't know what – told me to have a final look round. So I made another wide circuit of the ships. I was half-way round when one of the escorting warships spelt out a signal to me with its lamp. The message read, 'Suspicious aircraft to starboard.'

We flew on for a bit and sighted an aircraft about four miles away. It was flying very low, just above the sea, and on a steady course towards the convoy, taking good advantage of the very low cloud over the Atlantic. It was just a dot at first – but obviously a big fellow. I went on to have a look at him. Just as a precaution, I pulled down my front gun sights, and mentioned to my co-pilot that I had the stranger beautifully in my sights.

He suddenly let out an Irish yell. 'Hi! it's a blinking Condor!' he cried.

He was jolly well right, too. It was a Focke-Wulf Condor painted sea-green as camouflage. The big German was going straight for the convoy and was now only two miles from it.

The second pilot ran back to man the side gun of the Hudson. I went all out on the throttle and at 1,100 feet began to dive. Four hundred yards away I was wondering who would fire first. At that moment the German and I began firing simultaneously, but my front guns didn't seem to be doing him any damage.

The enemy's shooting was bad. Not one of his bullets or cannon shells hit us then or afterwards.

I brought my Hudson still lower and got into position 200 yards away to give my rear gunner a chance. He took it beautifully and promptly. I could see the tracer bullets from his tail gun whipping into the Focke-Wulf's two port engines and into its fuselage about mid-wing.

We got closer still – actually to between 20 and 30 feet – so close that the Focke-Wulf looked like a house. All the time my tail-gunner's tracers were still ripping into the Jerry. When there was only 8 yards between us we saw a gun poked out from a window of the Focke-Wulf. A face appeared above it, but it wasn't there long. The second pilot saw the face and spoiled it with a burst from one of his side guns.

By this time two of the four engines of the Focke-Wulf were in a glow. The German turned. As he did so he showed us his belly. My tail and side guns absolutely raked it.

I made a tight turn the other way. When the Hudson came out of it, I saw the German about a mile away still flying apparently all right. We know that these big Focke-Wulfs are built to give and take heavy punishment. But I was amazed that this fellow could still fly at all after the hiding we had given him.

I set off after him again, but the chase didn't last long. The Focke-Wulf soon crashed into the sea. It pancaked on the water, and we could see five members of its crew swimming from the wreckage and another one scampering along the fuselage.

We went round them a few times until we saw the six survivors hanging on to a rubber dinghy. The last we heard was that they were picked up by one of our warships.

We had a last look at the convoy. Every man on board the warships and merchant vessels, from captains to cooks, seemed to be on deck, waving and signalling their thanks for the grandstand view of the end of another Focke-Wulf.

My relief was now in sight and so I made for home.

9. NIGHT FIGHTER

OF THE 33 ENEMY RAIDERS DESTROYED LAST NIGHT
IT IS NOW ESTABLISHED THAT FOUR WERE BROUGHT
DOWN BY A.A. GUNS. THE REMAINING 29 FELL TO THE
GUNS OF THE R.A.F. NIGHT- FIGHTER PILOTS ... OUR
NIGHT-FIGHTING FORCES TOOK FULL ADVANTAGE OF
THE BRILLIANT MOONLIGHT. (Air Ministry Bulletin)

Try to imagine the moonlight sky, with a white background of snow nearly six miles below. Somewhere near the centre of a toy town a tiny flare is burning. Several enemy bombers have come over, but only one fire has gained a hold. After all the excitement of my two combats, I can still see that amazing picture of London clearly in my mind.

It was indeed the kind of night that we fly-by-nights pray for. I had been up about three-quarters of an hour before I found an enemy aircraft. I had searched all round the sky when I suddenly saw him ahead of me. I pulled the boost control to get the highest possible speed and catch him up. I felt my Hurricane vibrate all over as she responded and gave her maximum power. I manoeuvred into position where I could see the enemy clearly with the least chance of his seeing me. As I caught him up I recognised him – a Dornier 'flying pencil.' Before I spotted him I had been almost petrified with the cold. I was beginning to wonder if I should ever be able to feel my hands, feet or limbs again. But the excitement warmed me up.

He was now nearly within range and was climbing to 30,000 feet. I knew the big moment had come. I daren't take my eyes off him, but just to make sure that everything was all right I took a frantic glance round the 'office' – that's what we call the cockpit – and checked everything. Then I began to close in on the Dornier and found I was travelling much too fast. I throttled back and slowed up just in time. We were frighteningly close. Then I swung up, took aim, and fired my eight guns. Almost at once I saw little flashes of fire dancing along the fuselage and centre section. My bullets had found their mark.

I closed in again, when suddenly the bomber reared up in front of me. It was all I could do to avoid crashing into him. I heaved at the controls to prevent a collision, and in doing so I lost sight of him. I wondered if he was playing pussy and intending to jink away, come up on the other side and take a crack at me, or whether he was hard hit. The next moment I saw him going down below me with a smoke trail pouring out.

Some of you may have seen that smoke trail. I felt a bit disappointed, because it looked as if my first shots had not been as effective as they appeared. Again I pulled the boost control and went down after him as fast as I knew how. I dived from 30,000 feet to 3,000 feet at such a speed that the bottom panel of the aircraft cracked, and as my ears were not used to such sudden changes of pressure I nearly lost the use of one of the drums. But there was no time to think of these things. I had to get that bomber. Then as I came nearer I saw he was on fire. Little flames were flickering around his fuselage and wings. Just as I closed in again he jinked away in a steep climbing turn. I was going too fast again, so I pulled the stick back and went up after him in a screaming left-hand climbing turn. When he got to the top of his climb I was almost on him. I took sight very carefully and gave the button a quick squeeze. Once more I saw little dancing lights on his fuselage, but almost instantaneously they were swallowed in a burst of flames. I saw him twist gently earthwards and there was a spurt of fire as he touched the earth. He blew up and set a copse blazing.

I circled down to see if any of the crew had got out, and then I suddenly remembered the London balloon barrage, so I climbed up and set course for home.

I had time now to think about the action. My windscreen was covered with oil, which made flying uncomfortable, and I had a nasty feeling that I might have lost bits of my aircraft. I remembered seeing bits of Jerry flying past me. There were several good-sized holes in the fabric, which could have been caused only by hefty lumps of Dornier. Also the engine seemed to be running a bit roughly, but that turned out to be my imagination. Anyway I soon landed, reported what had happened, had some refreshment, and then up in the air once more, southward ho! for London.

Soon after I was at 17,000 feet. It's a bit warmer there than at 30,000. I slowed down and searched the sky. The next thing I knew, a Heinkel was sitting right on my tail. I was certain he had seen me, and wondered how long he had been trailing me. I opened my throttle, got round on his tail and crept up. When I was about 400 yards away he opened fire – and missed me. I checked my gadgets, then I closed up and snaked about so as to give him as difficult a target as possible. I got into a firing position, gave a quick burst of my guns and broke away.

I came up again, and it looked as if my shots had had no effect. Before I could fire a second time, I saw his tracer bullets whizzing past me. I fired back and I knew at once that I had struck home. I saw a parachute open up on the port wing. One of the crew was baling out. He was quickly followed by another. The round white domes of the parachutes looked lovely in the moonlight.

It was obvious now that the pilot would never get his aircraft home, and I, for my part, wanted this second machine to be a 'certainty' and not a 'probable.' So I gave another quick burst of my guns. Then to fool him I attacked from different angles. There was no doubt now that he was going down. White smoke was coming from one engine, but he was not yet on fire. I delivered seven more attacks, spending all my ammunition. Both his engines smoked as he got lower and lower. I followed him down a long way and as he flew over a dark patch of water I lost sight of him.

But I knew he had come down, and where he had come down – it was all confirmed later – and I returned to my base ready to tackle another one. But they told me all the Jerries had gone home. 'Not all,' I said, 'two of them are here for keeps.'

10. CANADA HITS THE TARGET

A CANADIAN SERGEANT – ONE OF THE FIRST BATCH
TO ARRIVE IN THIS COUNTRY UNDER THE EMPIRE
TRAINING SCHEME – TO-DAY SUNK A GERMAN SUPPLY
SHIP OF ABOUT 2,500 TONS WITH A DIRECT BOMB HIT
ON THE STERN. (Air Ministry Bulletin)

When I was training out in Canada we used to practise dropping small bombs on little wooden targets in Lake Ontario. And, of course, when we did so we all thought of the day when we would be dropping rather larger bombs on real targets with Germans in them. This thought didn't seem to improve my aim much, however, for try as hard as I could I never actually succeeded in scoring a direct hit on those little targets in Lake Ontario.

But the day I used to think about over in Canada has now arrived, and I am going to give you an account of it.

When we took off there weren't many clouds to give us cover, and as we got nearer to the Dutch coast the clouds grew fewer. We made our landfall and turned to fly along the coast towards the Hook. And there, about three miles out from the mouth of the river, we saw a German supply ship well down in the water as though she were carrying a heavy cargo. Because there was so little cloud cover, we were rather high up for bombing, but we decided to have a crack at it.

'We'll make a run over, anyway,' said the pilot, who incidentally is also a Canadian.

I got down to the bomb-sight and started to adjust it for height and drift, while the pilot made almost a perfect run up. I only had to give him one correction in course. The ship, by the way, was firing at us by then with the gun on her bows, and several shore batteries were opening up, too. Black clouds of high explosive were forming a little way from us. The first time I saw them I didn't realise what was happening.

'Those are funny looking clouds ahead of us,' I said to the pilot.

'Boy!' he replied, 'those aren't clouds!'

But to continue, I was adjusting my bomb-sight and everything seemed to fit in perfectly. Just as I got the final adjustments made the ship seemed to fall plump into the sights, so I released a single heavy bomb – the first bomb I had dropped over here. The ship swung round to take avoiding action and swung her stern right under the bomb. I saw it explode, a direct hit on the stern – which was more than I ever did to those little targets on Lake Ontario.

The explosion was followed by a big cloud of black smoke. I found myself shouting with excitement. The gunner too was singing out, 'It's a hit – it's a hit!' The pilot said, 'I do think you might have dropped it down her funnel.'

Then there was another explosion on the ship, with a cloud of white steam this time. Her boilers had burst. I know what that looks like, because I once saw a ship's boilers burst on the Canadian lakes when I was working as a steward on an excursion steamer in the summer, to pay my way through college in the Fall.

We did not have much time to enjoy our excitement, because just then the gunner called out a warning that there were two Messerschmitts coming. I looked down, and there they were, streaking up at us. So we climbed into some cloud and flew around until we figured we'd lost them.

But, just before we went into the cloud, the gunner saw that the ship was sinking rapidly by the stern.

Then we flew back to our base in England – and I had dropped my first bomb.

11. STARBOARD WING ON FIRE

THE KING HAS BEEN GRACIOUSLY PLEASED TO
CONFER THE VICTORIA CROSS ON THE
UNDERMENTIONED AIRMAN IN RECOGNITION OF
MOST CONSPICUOUS BRAVERY:
NZ/401793 SERGEANT — ROYAL NEW ZEALAND AIR
FORCE – NO. 75 (N.Z.) SQUADRON.
ON THE NIGHT OF 7TH JULY, 1941, SERGEANT — WAS
SECOND PILOT OF A WELLINGTON RETURNING FROM
AN ATTACK ON MUNSTER... (Air Ministry Bulletin)

It was on one of the Munster raids that it happened. It had been one of those trips that you dream about – hardly any opposition over the target; just a few searchlights but very little flak – and that night at Munster I saw more fires than I had ever seen before. We dropped our bombs right in the target area and then made a circuit of the town to see what was going on before the pilot set course for home.

As second pilot I was in the astro-dome keeping a look-out all round. All of a sudden, over the middle of the Zuider Zee, I saw an enemy machine coming in from port. I called up the pilot to tell him, but our inter-com. had gone phut. A few seconds later, before anything could be done about it, there was a slamming alongside us and chunks of red-hot shrapnel were shooting about all over the place.

As soon as we were attacked, the squadron leader who was flying the plane put the nose down to try and dive clear. At that time we didn't know that the rear gunner had got the attacking plane, a Messerschmitt 110, because the intercom. was still out of action and we couldn't talk to the rear turret.

We'd been pretty badly damaged in the attack. The starboard engine had been hit and the hydraulic system had been put out of action, with the result that the undercarriage fell half down, which meant, of course, that it would be useless for landing unless we could get it right down and locked. The bomb doors fell open too, the wireless sets were not working, and the front gunner was wounded in the foot. Worst of all, fire was burning up through the upper surface of the starboard wing where a petrol feed pipe had been split open. We all thought we'd have to bale out, so we put on our parachutes. Some of us got going with the fire extinguisher, bursting a hole in the side of the fuselage so that we could get at the wing, but the fire was too far out along the wing for that to be any good. Then we tried throwing coffee from our flasks at it, but that didn't work either. It might have damped the fabric round the fire, but it didn't put the fire out.

By this time we had reached the Dutch coast and were flying along parallel with it, waiting to see how the fire was going to develop.

The squadron leader said, 'What does it look like to you?' I told him the fire didn't seem to be gaining at all and that it seemed to be quite steady. He said, 'I think we'd prefer a night in the dinghy in the North Sea to ending up in a German prison camp.' With that he turned out seawards and headed for England.

I had a good look at the fire and I thought there was a sporting chance of reaching it by getting out through the astro-dome, then down the side of the fuselage and out on to the wing. Joe, the navigator, said he thought it was crazy. There was a rope there; just the normal length of rope attached to the rubber dinghy to stop it drifting away from the aircraft when it's released on the water. We tied that round my chest, and I climbed up through the astro-dome. I still had my parachute on. I wanted to take it off because I thought it would get in the way, but they wouldn't let me. I sat on the edge of the astro-dome for a bit with my legs still inside, working out how I was going to do it. Then I reached out with one foot and kicked a hole in the fabric so that I could get my foot into the framework of the plane, and then I punched another hole through the fabric in front of me to get a hand-hold, after which I made further holes and went down the side of the fuselage on to the wing. Joe was holding on to the rope so that I wouldn't sort of drop straight off.

I went out three or four feet along the wing. The fire was burning up through the wing rather like a big gas jet, and it was blowing back just past my shoulder. I had only one hand to work with getting out, because I was holding on with the other to the cockpit cover. I never realised before how bulky a cockpit cover was. The wind kept catching it and several times nearly blew it away and me with it. I kept bunching it under my arm. Then out it would blow again. All the time, of course, I was lying as flat as I could on the wing, but I couldn't get right down close because of the parachute in front of me on my chest. The wind kept lifting me off the wing. Once it slapped me back on to the fuselage again, but I managed to hang on. The slipstream from the engine made things worse. It was like being in a terrific gale, only much worse than any gale I've ever known in my life.

I can't explain it, but there was no sort of real sensation of danger out there at all. It was just a matter of doing one thing after another and that's about all there was to it.

I tried stuffing the cockpit cover down through the hole in the wing on to the pipe where the fire was starting from, but as soon as I took my hand away the terrific draught blew it out again and finally it blew away altogether. The rear gunner told me afterwards that he saw it go sailing past his turret. I just couldn't hold on to it any longer.

After that there was nothing to do but to get back again. I worked my way back along the wing, and managed to haul myself up on to the top of the fuselage and got to sitting on the edge of the astro-dome again. Joe kept the dinghy rope taut all the time, and that helped. By the time I got back I was absolutely done in. I got partly back into the astro-hatch, but I just couldn't get my right foot inside. I just sort of sat there looking at it until Joe reached out and pulled it in for me. After that, when I got inside, I just fell straight on to the bunk and stayed there for a time...

Just when we were within reach of the English coast the fire on the wing suddenly blazed up again. What had happened was that some petrol which had formed a pool inside the lower surface of the wing had caught fire. I remember thinking to myself, 'This is pretty hard after having got as far as this.' However, after this final flare-up the fire died right out – much to our relief, I can tell you.

The trouble now was to get down. We pumped the wheels down with the emergency gear and the pilot decided that, instead of going to our own base, he'd try to land at another aerodrome nearby which had a far greater landing space. As we circled before landing he called up the control and said, 'We've been badly shot up. I hope we shan't mess up your flare-path too badly when we land.' He put the aircraft down beautifully, but we ended up by running into a barbed-wire entanglement. Fortunately nobody was hurt though, and that was the end of the trip.

12. HAVOC STALKS HUN

FIGHTER COMMAND PILOTS IN AMERICAN-BUILT
HAVOC AIRCRAFT PAID VISITS TO GERMAN-OCCUPIED
AERODROMES IN NORTHERN FRANCE DURING THE
NIGHT. (Air Ministry Bulletin)

First of all, I should like to tell you not to measure the value of this night-fighter work over German aerodromes by the number of enemy aircraft known to have been destroyed. This is considerable, but I know positively that our mere presence over the enemy's bases has caused the loss of German bombers without even a shot being fired at them. Moreover, our presence upsets the *Luftwaffe* bomber organisation, throws their plans out of gear in many ways, and has a very big effect on the morale of the bomber crews.

Night-fighter pilots chosen for this work are generally of a different type to the ordinary fighter pilot. They must like night-fighting to begin with, which is not everybody's meat. They must also have the technique for blind flying, and when it comes to fighting, must use their own initiative and judgment, since they are cut off from all communications with their base and are left as free lances entirely to their own resources.

Personally I love it. Once up, setting a course in the dark for enemy-occupied country, one gets a tremendous feeling of detachment from the world. And when the enemy's air base is reached there is no thrill – even in big-game shooting – quite the same.

On goes the flare-path, a bomber comes low – making a circuit of the landing field – lights on and throttle shut. A mile or two away, in our stalking Havoc, we feel our hearts dance. The throttle is banged open, the stick thrust forward, and the Havoc is tearing down in an irresistible rush.

One short burst from the guns is usually sufficient. The bomber's glide turns to a dive – the last dive it is likely to make. Whether you get the Hun or miss him, he frequently piles up on the ground through making his landing in fright.

My own successes stand out clearly in my mind.

There was one night over France when I got an He. 111 for sure, and a Ju. 88 as a probable.

It was the night of the last big raid on London, and the Huns were streaming back to their bases in swarms. I got a crack at the Ju. as, with navigation lights on, it came down to land. The bullets appeared to enter the starboard engine and fuselage of the bomber. My onward rush carried us over the Ju., some ten feet above it, and as we passed my rear gunner poured a longish burst into the port engine. The bomber went into an almost vertical dive. She was only 800 feet up, and it is practically impossible that the pilot could have pulled out of the dive, apart from the fact that both his engines were damaged. But we only claimed the Ju. as a probable.

After this, all the aerodrome lights were turned off. We climbed away and the lights came on again. So we bombed the aerodrome, and large fires resulted. The aerodrome lights were again put out. But there were numerous bombers still trying to land. We came down to 1,000 feet again and met an He. 111. I opened fire close in. The bullets entered one engine and the fuselage. After a second burst smoke poured from both engines, and it went into a steep, side-slipping turn. As we passed beneath her, the gunner put in another burst.

Then, one night near St Leger, after we had bombed the aerodrome at Douai, we met a huge Focke-Wulf Condor, a four-engined transport. It had its navigation lights on, about to land. At only 50 yards range, I put a good burst into the transport's belly. It was all that was necessary.

The Condor gave out an enormous flash of light, burst into flames and blew to bits. Burning debris flew past my aircraft on all sides. When the Condor exploded in front of us, the flash was so blinding and the force was so great that we all thought our own machine had exploded.

My most recent thrill was a fortnight ago, when I got one enemy aircraft destroyed and damaged two others, over an aerodrome which I visited by chance. I happened to go that way, and was overjoyed to find myself there at the right moment. Only a few aircraft were operating that night from that vicinity, and I was able to have a crack at three of them.

13. WE SHADOWED THE 'BISMARCK'

THE FOLLOWING SIGNALS HAVE BEEN EXCHANGED IN
CONNECTION WITH THE 'BISMARCK' OPERATIONS
BETWEEN THE ADMIRALTY AND THE A.O.C.-IN-C.,
COASTAL COMMAND.
FROM ADMIRALTY TO THE AIR OFFICER
COMMANDING-IN-CHIEF, COASTAL COMMAND:
ADMIRALTY WISH GRATEFULLY TO ACKNOWLEDGE
THE PART PLAYED BY THE RECONNAISSANCE OF THE
FORCES UNDER YOUR COMMAND, WHICH
CONTRIBUTED IN A LARGE MEASURE TO THE
SUCCESSFUL OUTCOME OF THE RECENT OPERATION.
MESSAGE IN REPLY TO THE ABOVE.
TO ADMIRALTY FROM THE A.O.C.-IN-C., COASTAL
COMMAND:
YOUR MESSAGE VERY MUCH APPRECIATED AND HAS
BEEN REPEATED TO ALL CONCERNED. IT WAS A GREAT
HUNT AND WE ARE EAGER AND READY FOR MORE.
(Air Ministry Bulletin)

We left our base at 3.30 in the morning, and we got to the area we had to search at 9.45. It was a hazy morning with poor visibility, and our job was to contact with 'Bismarck,' which had been lost since early Sunday morning. About an hour later we saw a dark shape ahead in the mist. We were flying low at the time. I and the second pilot were sitting side by side and we saw the ship at the same time. At first we could hardly believe our eyes. I believe we both shouted, 'There she is,' or something of the sort.

There was a forty-knot wind blowing and a heavy sea running, and she was digging her nose right in, throwing it white over her bows. At first, as we weren't sure that it was an enemy battleship, we had to make certain. So we altered course, went up to about 1,500 feet into a cloud, and circled. We thought we were near the stern of her when the cloud ended, and there we were, right above her. The first we knew of it was a couple of puffs of smoke just outside the cockpit window, and a devil of a lot of noise. And then we were surrounded by dark brownish black smoke as she pooped off at us with everything she'd got. She'd only been supposed to have eight anti-aircraft guns, but fire was coming from more than eight places – in fact, she looked just one big flash. The explosions threw the flying-boat about, and we could hear bits of shrapnel hit the hull. Luckily only a few penetrated.

My first thought was that they were going to get us before we'd sent the signal off, so I grabbed a bit of paper and wrote out the message and gave it to the wireless operator. At the same time the second pilot took control, and took avoiding action. I should say that as soon as the 'Bismarck' saw us she'd taken avoiding action too, by turning at right angles, heeling over and pitching in the heavy sea.

When we'd got away a bit we cruised round while we inspected our damage. The rigger and I went over the aircraft, taking up floor-boards and thoroughly inspecting the hull. There were about half a dozen holes, and the rigger stopped them up with rubber plugs. We also kept an eye on the petrol gauges, because if they were going down too fast, that meant the tanks were holed and we wouldn't stand much chance of getting home. However, they were all right, and we went back to shadow 'Bismarck.' Then we met another Catalina. She'd been searching an area north of us, when she intercepted our signals and closed. On the way she'd seen a naval force, also coming towards us at full pelt through the heavy seas. They were part of our pursuing Fleet.

When we saw this Catalina we knew she was shadowing the ship from signals we'd intercepted and because she was going round in big circles. So I formated on him and went close alongside. I could see the pilot through the cockpit window and he pointed in the direction the 'Bismarck' was going. He had come to relieve us: it was just as well, for we couldn't stay much longer, because the holes in our hull made it essential to land in daylight. So we left the other Catalina to shadow 'Bismarck.' You all know what happened after that.

We landed just after half-past nine at night, after flying for over eighteen hours. But one of our Catalinas during this operation set up a new record for Coastal Command of twenty-seven hours on continuous reconnaissance.

14. W.A.A.F. IN AIR RAIDS

IT IS NOW COMMONPLACE TO HEAR THAT IN GERMAN
ATTACKS ON R.A.F. AERODROMES THE W.A.A.F.
PERSONNEL DISPLAYED GREAT COURAGE AND
COOLNESS... (Air Ministry Bulletin)

One cool, sunny morning I was talking to my senior sergeant (flight-sergeant) in the guard-room about the ordinary routine of the day, when the station broadcast ordered one squadron 'to come to readiness.' I told her that I might as well stay where I was for the time being, and go with her down one of the airwomen's trenches nearby should there prove to be a raid. But as the minutes passed and there were no further announcements, I started off towards my office in the station headquarters building.

As I entered headquarters the sirens wailed and we were told to go to the trenches. A few seconds later we heard one squadron roar into the air, then another, then still another, and finally the civilian air-raid warnings sounded in the surrounding country. We laughed and chatted on our way to the trenches, as this was no unusual occurrence.

We had hardly settled down when the noise of the patrolling aircraft overhead changed from a constant buzz to the zoom and groan of aircraft in a dog-fight. Then aircraft and machine-guns barked and sputtered, while plane after plane dove down with a head-splitting, nerve-shattering roar. I had no idea that so much could happen so quickly and remember thinking: 'I suppose one feels like this in a bad earthquake.'

Then there was a lull, broken only by the sound of our aircraft returning to refuel and re-arm. A moment later a messenger arrived to report that a trench had been hit on the edge of the aerodrome. The padre and another officer followed the messenger to the scene of the disaster, and I thought I'd better go and see if the airwomen were all right in their trenches. All was now deathly silent. I climbed through debris and round craters back towards the W.A.A.F. guard-room. As I drew nearer, there was a strong smell of escaping gas. The mains had been hit. Another bomb had fallen on the airwomen's trench near the guard-room, burying the women who were sheltering inside.

After a while I returned to headquarters to report to the Station Commander, and was told that the W.A.A.F. Officers' Mess could not be used as there was a delayed-action bomb in the garden.

After some food, I went over to the W.A.A.F. cookhouse to see how things were going. The airwomen's Mess was the only one which had not been damaged by the raid, and I could see that they would have to do all the cooking for the station for a bit. On the way there I saw something like a white pillow lying on the ground. As I approached to pick it up a voice said out of the darkness, 'I shouldn't touch that if I was you, Miss, it's marking a delayed-action bomb.' I thanked him very much, and trying hard not to look as though I was walking any quicker than I had been previously, I proceeded on my way to the cookhouse.

The airwomen were cooking virtually in the dark. But to their eternal credit they were producing delicious smelling sausages and mash to an endless stream of men going past a service hatch.

The next afternoon, as I was returning to the aerodrome from my 'billet-hunting' expedition with another W.A.A.F. officer, we were caught in a second attack. Our choices of action were few. There was no time to get to a trench, so we hurriedly put on our tin hats and ran into a nearby wood. As we did so, all the preliminary noises of the previous day began again. The edge of the wood was near a cross-roads, and as we ducked under the trees the police 'bell-shelter' opened and a policeman shouted, 'You'd better come in here.' We did not hesitate, but scrambled in quickly. It was a tight squeeze, but it became much worse when a bus-driver, who also wanted admission, banged on the door. Somehow – I still don't know how – we got him inside.

We waited till the noise had died down before we emerged, weighing, I am sure, much less. By the time we reached the aerodrome a fierce fire was raging in one quarter, but this time all my airwomen had escaped injury.

This story covers a period of almost forty-eight hours. It started with a clean, tidy station, efficient to perfection; it ends with buildings destroyed, telephone lines blown up, and the aerodrome itself cratered. But not for one second did this station cease to be operational; it never failed to keep open its communications, and it still got fed! For their heroic work three of my airwomen were later awarded Military Medals.

15. DOG-FIGHTS OVER ENGLAND

THE KING HAS BEEN GRACIOUSLY PLEASED TO
APPROVE THE FOLLOWING AWARDS IN RECOGNITION
OF GALLANTRY DISPLAYED IN FLYING OPERATIONS
AGAINST THE ENEMY:
BAR TO THE DISTINGUISHED FLYING CROSS.
ACTING WING COMMANDER —, D.S.O., D.F.C. THIS
FEARLESS PILOT HAS RECENTLY ADDED A FURTHER
FOUR ENEMY AIRCRAFT TO HIS PREVIOUS SUCCESSES;
IN ADDITION, HE HAS PROBABLY DESTROYED
ANOTHER FOUR AND DAMAGED FIVE HOSTILE
AIRCRAFT... (Air Ministry Bulletin)

I'd like to tell you something about the boys in my squadron. They're grand lads, every one of them. About 75 per cent. are Canadians and many of them came over to this country a year or two before the war to join the R.A.F. Several worked their way across, at least two of them on cattle-boats, and they all came here to do what they'd wanted to do since they were youngsters – to fly.

Since the war started they've shown that they can fight as well as they fly, and between them they've already won six of the nine D.F.C.s which have been awarded to the squadron. One holder of the D.F.C. is from Victoria, British Columbia. Another, who has won a bar to his D.F.C., comes from Calgary, Alberta. Others come from Toronto, Vancouver and Saskatoon. There's never been a happier or more determined crowd of fighter pilots, and, as an Englishman, I'm very proud to have the honour of leading them.

I shan't soon forget the first time the squadron was in action under my leadership. It was on August 30th, and I detailed the pilot from Calgary to take his section of three Hurricanes up to keep thirty Me. 110's busy. 'O.K., O.K.,' he said with obvious relish, and away he streaked to deal with that vastly superior number of enemy fighters. When I saw him afterwards, his most vivid impression was of one German aircraft which he had sent crashing into a greenhouse. But perhaps I'd better start at the beginning of that particular day's battle.

Thirteen of the squadron were on patrol near London. We were looking for the Germans whom we knew were about in large formations.

Soon we spotted one large formation, and it was rather an awe-inspiring sight – particularly to anyone who hadn't previously been in action. I counted fourteen blocks of six aircraft – all bombers – with thirty Me. 110 fighters behind and above. So that altogether there were more than 100 enemy aircraft to deal with.

Four of the boys had gone off to check up on some unidentified aircraft which had appeared shortly before we sighted the big formation, and they weren't back in time to join in the fun. That left nine of us to tackle the big enemy formation. I sent three Hurricanes up to keep the 110's busy, while the remaining six of us tackled the bombers. They were flying at 15,000 feet with the middle of the formation roughly over Enfield, heading east. When we first sighted them they looked just like a vast swarm of bees. With the sun at our backs and the advantage of greater height, conditions were ideal for a surprise attack and as soon as we were all in position we went straight down on to them.

We didn't adopt any set rule in attacking them – we just worked on the axiom that the shortest distance between two points is a straight line. I led the attack and went for what I think was the third block of six from the back. And *did* those Huns break up! In a few seconds there was utter confusion. They broke up all over the sky. As I went through, the section I aimed at fanned out. I can't give you an exact sequence of events, but I know that the Canadian pilot who followed immediately behind took the one that broke away to the left, while I took the one that broke away to the right. The third man in our line went straight through and gave the rear gunner of a Hun in one of the middle blocks an awful shock. Then the other boys followed on and things really began to get moving.

Now there's one curious thing about this air fighting. One minute you see hundreds of aeroplanes in the sky, and the next minute there's nothing. All you can do is to look through your sights at your particular target – and look in your mirror too, if you are sensible, for any Messerschmitts which might be trying to get on to your tail.

Well, that particular battle lasted about five or ten minutes, and then, quite suddenly, the sky was clear of aircraft. We hadn't shot them all down, of course; they hadn't waited for that, but had made off home in all directions at high speed.

When we got down we totted up the score. We had destroyed twelve enemy aircraft with our nine Hurricanes. And when we examined our aircraft there wasn't a single bullet-hole in any of them!

One pilot had sent a Hun bomber crashing into a greenhouse. Another bomber had gone headlong into a field filled with derelict motor-cars. It hit one of the cars, turned over and caught fire. Another of our chaps had seen a twin-engined job of sorts go into a reservoir near Enfield. Yet another pilot saw his victim go down with his engine flat out. The plane dived into a field and disintegrated into little pieces. Incidentally, that particular pilot brought down three Huns that day. Apart from our bag of twelve, there were a number of others which were badly shot up and probably never got home, like one which went staggering out over Southend with one engine out of action.

Another day we like to remember – what fighter squadron who was in the show doesn't! – was Sunday, September 15th, when 185 enemy aircraft were destroyed. Our squadron led a wing of four or five squadrons in two sorties that day, and we emerged with 52 victims for the Wing, twelve of them falling to our squadron.

On the first show that day we were at 20,000 feet, and ran into a large block of Ju. 88's and Do. 17's – about forty in all and without a single fighter to escort them. This time, for a change, we outnumbered the Hun, and believe me, no more than eight got home from that party. At one time you could see planes going down on fire all over the place, and the sky seemed full of parachutes. It was sudden death that morning, for our fighters shot them to blazes.

One unfortunate German rear-gunner baled out of the Dornier 17 I attacked, but his parachute caught on the tail. There he was, swinging helplessly, with the aircraft swooping and diving and staggering all over the sky, being pulled about by the man hanging by his parachute from the tail. That bomber went crashing into the Thames Estuary, with the swinging gunner still there.

Just about the same time one of my boys saw a similar thing in another Dornier, though this time the gunner who tried to bale out had his parachute caught before it opened. It caught in the hood, and our pilot saw the other two members of the crew crawl up and struggle to set him free. He was swinging from his packed parachute until they pushed him clear. Then they jumped off after him, and their plane went into the water with a terrific smack. I've always thought it was a pretty stout effort on the part of those two Huns who refused to leave their pal fastened to the doomed aircraft.

The other day I led two of the latest recruits to the squadron on a search for a Ju. 88 off the East Coast. We found it fifty or sixty miles out to sea, and I led an attack from below. Suddenly the raider jettisoned his bombs and two of us had to duck out of the way. We know some of the German tricks to try to get rid of our fighters, and at first I thought he was throwing out some new kind of secret weapon to bump us off. Then I realised he'd let them go to help his speed.

I kept with him and told the other two boys to go in and have a crack. Their shooting was amazingly accurate, and for the first time I saw bullets other than my own going into the fuselage of an enemy bomber. You know how the lights flash on a penny-in-the-slot bagatelle table? As the little ball goes through the various pins different lights flash. Well, that's how the bullets from one of these Hurricanes went in.

I watched them cracking in. The bomber pilot tried to get away and made for a cloud about the size of a man's hand. He went in, while one of my boys cruised around on top and the other waited underneath. Either the pilot of that Ju. 88 was a damned fool or he just couldn't help it, but he came flying nicely out of the cloud at the other end on a straight course. The boy on top nipped down on him like a greyhound after a hare. The boy below went up – it was almost like watching an event at a coursing meeting. When they had finished their ammunition those two Canadians left the bomber in a pretty bad state, and all I had to do was to finish him off.

16. LOW-LEVEL RAID ON NANTES

THE PEOPLE OF NANTES HEARD A MESSAGE OF HOPE
AND ULTIMATE DELIVERANCE FOR FRANCE ON SUNDAY
NIGHT WHEN A FORCE OF BEAUFORTS OF THE COASTAL
COMMAND FLEW LOW OVER THE CITY AS DUSK FELL.
THE TOWN IS SURROUNDED BY GERMAN TROOPS AND
IS WHERE THE 50 HOSTAGES ARE IN PRISON. OUR
AIRCRAFT DROPPED A LOAD OF HIGH-EXPLOSIVE AND
INCENDIARY BOMBS ON THE DOCKS AREA AND ALSO
DISTRIBUTED THOUSANDS OF LEAFLETS TO THE
CITIZENS OF NANTES. (Air Ministry Bulletin)

The flight over the sea to France was thrilling. We flew in formation over the waves at about 100 feet. The seas were running high and we passed over trawlers which were literally standing on their tails.

So it was a great relief when we arrived. We were so low when we reached the French coast that I had to pull up sharply to avoid the sand-dunes. There was still some daylight and we went along at what we call 'nought feet.' Every time we came to a clump of trees we leap-frogged over them and then went down almost to the ground again. We went over scores of little villages and we could see the people open their doors and rush to wave.

It grew darker as we went farther inland, and then began the most surprising experience of all. It was really remarkable – as though the whole of that part of France were turning out to welcome us.

Every village we went over became a blaze of light. People threw open their doors and came out to watch us skim their chimney-pots. In other places whole hamlets would suddenly light up, as if the people had torn the blackout down when they heard us coming and had waited until we were overhead to switch on the lights.

Sometimes people switched their lights on and off until we had gone over. I remember one house with a courtyard fully lit up. I saw a woman come out of the house, look up at us, wave, and then go back. She switched off the outside lights and then I saw a yellow light from inside stream out as she opened the door.

Our targets were the docks on the banks of the River Loire. The moon was up now, but it was only shining fitfully through a cloud. Still, we could see the river easily enough, and the other Beauforts formated on me until we separated near the target as we had planned.

It was a good moment as we ran up over the docks of Nantes outside the town. The squadron had thrown every effort into this raid. It was the climax as we climbed 200 or 300 feet above the water and let the bombs go in a shallow dive.

I followed my bombs down until I was just above the ground again, and then I beat it, flat out, across the roof-tops of Nantes.

The whole city was laid out below us, church spires gleaming in the moonlight, streets and houses clearly outlined. It looked like a city of the dead for the first minute.

Then I began to see white pin-points on the ground, and one by one lights appeared as we raced over the chimney-pots, our engines flat out and creating a terrific roar. We were at top speed, but even so we could see doors opening and people coming out.

I felt that we had brought some comfort to the people of Nantes and that they had come out to wave and wish us good luck.

17. PARACHUTE TROOPS

BEFORE THE AIRCRAFT HAD DISAPPEARED INTO
CLOUD AGAIN, THEY HAD LANDED, UNHARNESSED
THEIR PARACHUTES, AND WERE SILENTLY PREPARING
TO ATTACK A REMOTE AND VITAL ENEMY OBJECTIVE.
(Air Ministry Bulletin)

It was the Russians who first translated the idea of the parachute – an idea first recorded by Leonardo da Vinci – into a means of war-like attack. The first parachute descent was 150 years ago, the first jump from an aeroplane thirty years ago, but it was not till about ten years ago that we began to see those pictures from Moscow – a thousand parachutes dappling a cloudless sky like spots on a silk handkerchief.

Reactions were various but the Germans alone methodically studied it, worked out their own rather different technique and adopted it for their young army. When they attacked Finland, the Russian parachute troops were almost a complete failure.

When the Germans attacked Norway, they tried their new technique. In a few cases they achieved their object and many lessons were learnt. It was in Holland that the parachutists were first successful. Comparatively few were used – perhaps 2,000 in all – and the main attacks were on The Hague and Rotterdam. All over the country was a well-organised mass of fifth-columnists.

Even so, the parachutists were not successful everywhere – certainly not at The Hague. But they showed the effect, both on civilian morale and on military organisation, of packets of armed men delivered by air far in advance of the main army.

One of the principal roles of parachute troops was clearly shown in Holland. They were the advance guard of much larger air-borne forces carried in troop-carrier aircraft. They dropped round selected points and held these till the Ju. 52's arrived. The theory of the air-borne force of all arms – the real flying column – was demonstrated for the first time. And the Germans, at least, were satisfied, for since then they have worked feverishly at the creation of a large air-borne army, numbered not by battalions but by divisions, to be transported in troop-carrying aircraft and in gliders, and of this force the paratroops are only a small proportion.

The proposed use of the German air-borne army is a matter of conjecture. If it is thrown against this country, its casualties will be terrific. But will they be greater than if the same troops were advancing across no-man's-land behind a barrage towards a trench line bristling with machine-guns? Probably not, and such attacks were sometimes successful in

Flanders. Perhaps this, then, will be Hitler's secret invasion weapon. I think we must prepare ourselves to make the most of this – the best opportunity we shall get of destroying a war-worshipping section of the enemy's forces that is particularly dear to their leaders.

Perhaps I may seem to have spoken unduly of the work of our enemies in the new field of air-borne warfare. What about ours? Some of you will have noticed on the arms of certain officers and men a very attractive badge with the white parachute between blue soaring wings. The recent small operation in Italy has shown the extent to which the joint work of the R.A.F. and the Army has developed this new art. I daresay that in the whole of Army Co-operation Command there is no better example of co-operation between the services than in the organisation and training of the Special Air Service troops that has been quietly taking place for some time.

The Royal Air Force has had to produce the parachute equipment, the methods of dropping and training, and to teach the troops all their air technique. Meanwhile, the Army have had to study the special organisation for fighting on the ground, the weapons and tactical training of the paratroops. Starting with the men themselves, they must be picked specimens, keen and determined and intelligent. It's going to cost a packet to get them on to the job, so when they get there, each of them must give the best possible account of himself. So, your parachutist is not the ape-faced all-in wrestler with a cauliflower ear, but a daring and clever man who feels that the only way to get the Germans down is to take the offensive, and who wants to do it as soon as possible.

He must be physically very fit. The effect of reaching the ground on a parachute is about the same as jumping from a 10-foot wall, the height of an average ceiling. And if there's some wind and the parachute is drifting and swinging a bit, it's as if he were jumping on to the deck of a ship that is steaming full speed and rolling and pitching as well, with its deck covered with fences and hedges and trees as well as fields. Pretty exciting!

The actual jump from the aircraft is specially important. The machine may be travelling over the ground at a couple of miles a minute. So, unless the men pop out of it very quickly, you can imagine that they'll land a long way apart from each other, and some will not be in the right place at all. Jumping in quick succession means careful drill.

The job of flying the troops into the exact position for dropping is a Royal Air Force responsibility, as well as the whole organisation of the air side of an operation. Skilful piloting and accurate judgment are needed, and this is what makes an air-borne attack the perfect example of co-operation between airmen and soldiers.

Our men, of course, always wear uniform. They are normal soldiers as much as the cavalry of the last generation, but they have special boots and helmets designed to give protection while landing, and their outer overalls, worn outside everything but their parachute harness, ensures that none of their equipment can catch in any part of the plane as they jump. Their weapons also are specially selected according to the job they have to do. Often they must fight rapidly at short range like gangsters; sometimes silently hand to hand...

Such troops offer a means of local attack on vital points – as it were of sticking a hypodermic into specially sensitive places in the enemy's anatomy. I was one of those who helped to prepare and organise the recent expedition to Italy, and I was later privileged to go out with it and occupy a front seat in the stalls throughout the performance. There could be no greater contrast than between the troops who took part in that and the Nazi paratroop thugs. They were, of course, a specially selected and trained force, expert in the particular work they had to do, carrying very special equipment and led by magnificent officers. Unfortunately, I may not give many interesting details of the attack that you would like to hear. That must come later. But I can say that the R.A.F. pilots and crews who carried the force did their job with characteristic thoroughness and accuracy. The flights were long, at night, a good deal over hostile territory, and for long periods in pretty bad weather, and the places they were navigating to were pin-points. But they just ran to schedule.

The night of the show itself was one of the most beautiful you can imagine: full moon and glorious stars above patches of white cloud; the sea clear of mist, and the snow-capped ridges of the Apennines. I'd flown over that bit of coast years ago in a Moth on my way to Africa and I could easily recognise it in the moonlight. It was a lovely scene. We could recognise every feature and landmark as we came in, looking just like the landscape model we had used in planning the job and training the air crews. It was easy afterwards to see the parachutes on the ground and the figures of the troops moving together, and giving us a last flash of their torches as we passed overhead.

It was a moment one will never forget; but even more I shall remember the efficiency and the wonderful spirit of the men we dropped, their bearing, and the way they got into the aircraft at the take-off, singing a song with special words of their own, not particularly suited to the B.B.C., the refrain of which was 'Oh! We've a surprise for the Duce, the Duce!' They certainly had, and perhaps not the last.

18. FORTRESS CROSSES THE ATLANTIC

A NUMBER OF THE VERY LATEST TYPE OF FOUR-
ENGINED FLYING FORTRESS BOMBERS HAVE JUST
REACHED THIS COUNTRY FROM THE UNITED STATES…
…DESPITE THEIR VAST SIZE, THE FLYING FORTRESSES
HAVE BEATEN ALL RECORDS IN THEIR FLIGHT ACROSS
THE ATLANTIC. THESE MACHINES WILL SHORTLY BE
FLYING ALONGSIDE BRITISH AND OTHER TYPES OF
UNITED STATES FOUR-ENGINED BOMBERS IN SERVICE
WITH THE ROYAL AIR FORCE. (Ministry of Aircraft Production)

I can't help feeling that there is not much of a story in this. The most remarkable thing about the whole flight was that it seemed so ordinary and uneventful. We just stepped into the Fortress on the other side one evening, flew her east all night, and landed in Britain soon after dawn the next day. It's true we had flown the Atlantic, but until we got close in to the British coast, we didn't even see the Atlantic. We were much too high. All we saw was the sky and the stars and the moon, clouds towering high above us here and there and a great floor of clouds beneath us. It was just about as exciting as a night flight from London to Paris in peacetime.

I happened to be in Canada doing a course – and a very good time the Canadians gave us, too. When the course was finished I was told that I was to fly as navigator in one of the American bombers being sent to this country, but I wasn't told what aircraft it would be. In fact, it was only a few hours before we took off that I went down to the aerodrome and had a look at the Fortress which had just arrived. There were some Liberators about too, and they were all being sent here to take part in the war.

I didn't actually get into the Fortress until just before we took off on the first stage of the journey from Montreal to Newfoundland. There wasn't much of a ceremony. A young lieutenant in the Canadian Army came down to wave us off and wish us luck. He seemed very impressed by the size of the Fortress – it really is a very large bomber indeed. And his last words to us were, 'She'll look nice over Berlin!'

After we left him we settled ourselves in for the journey and I had a good look round the aircraft. My own 'office,' as navigator, was up in the nose. It was quite big enough to be called an office. It had a nice big table in it, a chair, plenty of lockers, and racks and instruments and a carpet on the floor. If I put my feet up to the table and leant back in the chair, I could just touch the opposite wall by stretching out my arm to its full length. And up in front a couple of machine guns stuck out, so that I could fight a bit of the war, if the need arose, almost without getting out of my office chair!

There was a window behind me through which I could pass messages up to the two pilots. The flight engineer sat behind them, and through the door at his back you got into the part of the fuselage where the bombs are carried. Through that, there was a catwalk leading aft to the fairly large room which housed the wireless operator and the gunners.

The whole thing was beautifully fitted out. The American Army fliers do themselves very well. They even have a sort of electric oven which is wheeled out of the hangar at the last minute, full of hot food, and plugged into the aircraft's electric circuit, to keep it hot. And behind the wireless operator there are two large urns with taps, one pouring out coffee, the other tea. But we weren't going far, so we contented ourselves with a few egg and bacon sandwiches and a few thermos flasks.

We reached our intermediate aerodrome in time for lunch, and in time, too, to watch two other Flying Fortresses set off for Britain. I've never seen such a place for snow. It had been cleared from the aerodrome, but it lay ten feet deep alongside, and it was melting and trickling over the runway, so that the two Fortresses took off in great clouds of spray kicked up behind them. They took off splendidly, though, and headed east.

We were held up for a couple of days by bad weather reports, so it was two evenings later, just as the sun was setting, that we, too, started out on the long flight to Britain.

There was a slight check soon after we started, for the wireless seemed to falter, and we turned to put back. But it righted itself and we turned again to the east, climbing at once to 20,000 feet, and staying at that height all the way over.

The journey was then quite uneventful. Once I strolled aft to see the wireless operator, but I found even that short walk took it out of me badly, and I was glad to get back to my own office and my oxygen supply. I spent most of the time navigating by the stars, and that kept me quite busy. Occasionally I chatted with the pilots, and I ate the sandwiches I had brought with me, and drank the tea from my flask. The bomber rode beautifully, with never a jolt. Far below us in the darkness was the cloud bank over the Atlantic. Sometimes we passed under a roof of cirrus cloud 5,000 feet or more above us. When the moon came up, it grew quite bright. It also grew extremely cold, and the temperature went down to about 45 degrees of frost, so that sometimes the windows were clouded over with hoar frost. And then my office, with the electric light shining on the table, the charts, the instruments, the rack of pencils, became a little room quite boxed away from the world, speeding steadily eastwards towards the war at 20,000 feet above the Atlantic.

Dawn was breaking as we approached the shores of Britain, and we started to come down through about 15,000 feet of cloud. A little ice formed on the wings as we came down, but nothing to worry us. Now and then one of us shone an electric torch through the window to keep an eye on the ice.

And then, in the thin torchlight, we could see the big wings of the Fortress stretching out into nothing, and the four engines turning steadily.

We broke cloud at about 1,500 feet above the sea. It started to grow light quickly then, and soon we were above the British coast – we came out, actually, only five miles from the point at which we were aiming.

The Group Captain of the aerodrome came out to meet us when we landed and took us in to a large and much-needed breakfast. The flight was over. Britain had another big bomber – just one more in the procession which is steadily moving eastwards now over the Atlantic.

19. HOME ON ONE ENGINE

WITH GREAT SKILL, SERGEANT — FLEW HIS SEVERELY
DAMAGED AIRCRAFT BACK TO THIS COUNTRY, AFTER
DROPPING HIS BOMBS ON AN ENEMY OBJECTIVE,
MAKING A SUCCESSFUL LANDING AT AN AERODROME,
WITHOUT INJURY TO THE CREW. (Air Ministry Bulletin)

Unlike the Germans, who only have to cross the Channel to get to
England, we have the North Sea to think of on our way to and from
Germany. And there have, of course, been plenty of adventures over the
North Sea in this way. I'll tell you now about one which happened to me and
my crew recently.

We had just made a successful night raid on the docks at
Wilhelmshaven and were barely ten minutes away from the target when
we ran into heavy anti-aircraft fire. It wasn't as bad as I have known it, but
one of the shells hit the starboard engine and soon after that the airscrew
came away from the engine and flew off into space. I didn't actually see it
go, and the first I knew that something was wrong was when the aircraft
swerved to the right – fortunately not a very violent swerve – and at the
same time I heard the navigator telling me what had happened.

I looked down and there were sparks and flames shooting out of the
engine cowling, and for a second or two I thought that it was all up with
us. I gave the crew the order to stand by to abandon aircraft, and then it
passed through my mind that we ought to be able to make a forced landing
in Germany. My next thought was that, either way, we'd become prisoners
of war, and I didn't like the idea of that at all.

By now the crew were ready to bale out, and then I saw that the flames
had disappeared. What put them out I don't know. The main thing is that
they went out, and with the danger of fire over, there was a reasonable
chance of getting back home. Anyhow, it was worth the gamble, and the
crew were, like me, all in favour of having a shot at it.

At the time we were 8,000 feet up, facing a strong headwind which
would soon have been too much for the single engine we had left – we would
have gone so slowly that we might not have got there. So I came down to
3,000 feet in a gentle glide. I'd been told before we set out that, at 3,000 feet,
the wind was less fierce. It was. The 'Met' section was right as usual.

The next problem was up to the rest of the crew rather than to me – that
was to try and lighten the machine. So I told the navigator, the wireless
operator, and the rear gunner to jettison everything that could be spared out of
the machine. This might lighten it and give us a chance to keep at a fairly good
height. Just before this the navigator, who sits in front and below the pilot, had

the bright idea of tying his oxygen tube round the left end of my rudder bar and pulling forward on it. This relieved me of a great deal of strain as, before, I had to correct the pull of our one engine all the time with the rudder. The navigator's brain-wave helped me out with the rudder and stopped me from getting cramp in the leg, though it didn't stop me from getting a nasty pain in the small of the back. It was a grand bit of quick thinking, and as soon as I was easier he got busy chucking things out of his own compartment. Guns, pans of ammunition and a good deal of our navigation equipment went into the sea. We kept just a few pans of ammunition as well as a couple of guns just in case we met an enemy. Next, the crew tried to get rid of the armour plating behind me, but it wouldn't budge. Then they tried to unship part of the bombing apparatus, but that was just as obstinate. By now we were down to 800 feet, but by getting rid of the guns and things we were able to keep at that height and later even climb to just over 1,000 feet.

Still there was always the danger of being forced down into the water, so the crew decided to get the dinghy ready in case it was wanted. We were keeping a reasonable air speed, but the one good engine was getting overheated. As dawn broke we could see no sign of land, though the navigator was confident that it wasn't far away. He was right, although at five minutes past seven we had only 35 gallons of petrol left and still no land to be seen. And then, only a few minutes later, the grey outline of the East Coast came in sight. It was too early to count our chickens but, when we crossed the coast thirty-five minutes afterwards, I knew we would be all right – if we could find an aerodrome. Then the navigator suddenly exclaimed, 'It's all right, there's an aerodrome a couple of miles away!' His navigation had been marvellous. He had reckoned with all the wobbling about I had done on the way and had brought us safely home. Down we went to make a perfect landing, four hours after the airscrew had said goodbye to the bomber. There was no petrol left in the tanks but, as you can imagine, our spirits were high.

20. HURRICANE BOMBER

AIRCRAFT OF FIGHTER COMMAND THIS AFTERNOON
CARRIED OUT A NUMBER OF OFFENSIVE PATROLS AND
SWEEPS OVER NORTHERN FRANCE AND THE COASTS
OF HOLLAND AND BELGIUM. HURRICANES CARRYING
BOMBS TOOK PART IN ONE OF THESE OPERATIONS.
(Air Ministry Communiqué)

Whoever thought of fitting bombs to a Hurricane is to be thanked for giving the squadron which I command some of the most thrilling days' work that has ever fallen to the luck of Fighter Command pilots.

Low-level bombing of ground targets by fighters which it makes possible is, of course, something quite new to R.A.F. pilots. In our Hurricane bombers we don't have to dive on to our targets. We come down almost to ground level before we reach them, and drop our bombs in level flight, with greater accuracy than can be achieved generally in dive-bombing.

The whole thrill of the Hurribomber is in this ground-level flying over the target. There we are, like a close formation of cars sweeping along the 'railway straight' at Brook lands, only, instead of fast car speeds, we are batting along at between 200 and 250 miles an hour. At times we may exceed 300 m.p.h.

The impression and thrill of speed near the ground has to be experienced to be believed. Even though we are travelling so fast, there would be a risk of being hurt by the blast of our own bombs if they were of the ordinary type which burst on contact. Consequently our bombs are fitted with delayed-action fuses, so that they do not explode until we have got well outside their blast range.

It might seem that, flying on to the target at only a few feet altitude, we would be easy prey for Bofors or machine-gun posts. We would be if the gunners could see us coming. But generally they cannot see the low-flying fighter until it is almost overhead, and then they have to be remarkably quick to get the gun trained on the fleeting aircraft. More-over, they have little time to calculate what deflections to allow in their aim. On the other hand, of course, the pilot would have precious little chance of baling out if his aircraft were hit. Indeed, he would have practically no space in which to regain control of his aircraft if a hit threw him temporarily out of gear.

So far, however, the advantage seems to be on our side, and not on the side of ground defences. I have seen 'flak' and machine-gun fire pelting at my aircraft from all angles, but none of it has hit me. We get intimate, if lightning, pictures of the countryside. People on the road, soldiers scrambling for cover, bombs bursting and throwing up debris around us.

Our first big day out recently was typical of the work of this new weapon of ours. We went over in half a gale. The target we were looking for eluded us on this particular occasion. I think we passed it only a mile to one side. We did a circuit, and not seeing our main target, began to look for our alternative.

I found myself flying down a river with a main line railroad running alongside. Ahead was a bridge, carrying the railway over the river. I called to my companion that I would bomb the bridge, and together we swept over it, barely skimming the structure, and let our bombs go.

Another pair in the squadron coming on behind saw the bombs explode in the river and the whole bridge slump to one side. As they passed over it, they saw the bridge looking as crooked as an eel.

I looked back to see the effect of our bombs, but all I saw was a string of tracer bullets going up behind my port wing. As I turned again, I saw it was coming from a gun-post on an aerodrome which my companion and I were already traversing. I was half-way across it before I recognised it as an aerodrome, but I was in time to give some huts on the far edge a good burst from my guns. After this I made for the coast again, flying slap over a town and straight down one of its main streets. The squadron reassembled just off the coast, and we beat it back to our base.

Altogether, it was what you'd call a party – or a rough house, according to whether you were at the receiving or the delivery end. And the only damage we sustained was a hole in a tailplane – and that was caused by a seagull!

21. R.A.A.F. TO THE RESCUE

A VÉRY CARTRIDGE SAVED THE LIVES OF A CREW OF A
R.A.F. AIRCRAFT, WHEN THEY WERE DRIFTING IN THEIR
RUBBER DINGHY IN THE SEA OFF THE SOUTH-WEST
COAST OF BRITAIN. THE CREW WERE FOUND BY A
SEARCHING HUDSON, LOST, AND FOUND AGAIN. AND A
FEW MINUTES LATER THEY WERE PICKED UP BY A
SUNDERLAND FLYING-BOAT OF AN AUSTRALIAN
SQUADRON OF THE R.A.F. COASTAL COMMAND, WHICH
ALIGHTED, AND TAXIED UP TO THEM. (Air Ministry Bulletin)

It was my flying-boat which picked up the Whitley boys from the
Atlantic, but we only came in at the end of the job. If it hadn't been for
a spot of good navigation by the Whitley crew themselves, and then by the
Hudsons, these lads would never have been found at all.

The Whitley crew sent out their position so exactly when they came
down, and the Hudson navigators worked so well, that the leading Hudson
was over the dinghy, dropping a bag of comforts, only fifty-nine minutes
after taking off. In the comforts bag that was dropped were food, brandy
and cigarettes. That's one way to get a smoke these days.

We in the Sunderland were flying towards the last-known position of
the dinghy. Then my wireless operator intercepted a message from one of
the Hudsons:

'Am over dinghy, in position so-and-so.'

We altered course for the new position, and at last came upon two
Hudsons circling round in steep turns. Soon we got close enough to see the
dinghy on the water. It was a dinghy made for only two men, but there
were six in it. They gave us a cheer as we went over.

We cracked off a signal to base that we were over them, and then I
began to wonder about getting down to pick them up. It's a tricky business
putting a big flying-boat down on a roughish sea in the Atlantic. A heavy
wave can easily smash the wing-tip floats, or even knock out an engine as
you touch down.

We flew around, talking it over, and looking very hard at the sea. It
wasn't too promising. The waves were about eight feet from trough to
crest. But there was one good point – the wind was blowing along the
swell, and not across it.

We soon decided to have a try, and I picked out a comparatively smooth
piece of water, about a mile from the dinghy. We landed all right. It was a
bit bumpy, but it was all right.

The next problem was to get the boys out of the dinghy and into the
flying-boat. We taxied near to them. Two of my crew clambered into one

of our own dinghies, at the end of a rope, and tried to paddle across to the Whitley dinghy.

But the rope was too short.

We tied another piece of rope on the end. It was still too short, even then.

One of my crew then climbed out on the Sunderland's wing and fastened the end of the rope to the wing-tip. But by that time the Whitley dinghy had drifted away, out of reach.

Then I thought we would tow our dinghy up to the Whitley's dinghy. We started up the engines, and moved off slowly, pulling our own dinghy along behind us. I'm afraid the lads in my dinghy got a bit wet.

After a few minutes we brought both the dinghies together. They floated alongside the Sunderland itself.

The Whitley dinghy seemed to be very crowded. When I took the crew aboard, I learned that their big dinghy had failed. So all of them had had to cram into the smaller one, which is designed to hold only two men.

We pulled them aboard through the after-hatch of the Sunderland – and just about time, too. Their dinghy was gradually filling with water, and I doubt whether it would have lived through the night. It was only half an hour before dusk when we picked them up.

They were quite all right, though. Just a bit tired. We gave them some hot tea and some food, and they turned in for a sleep on the way home.

We did get one bit of amusement before we got back to base… About thirty miles off the coast we saw beneath us one of the high-speed rescue launches, haring out towards the position where we had picked up the crew.

We flashed a signal to the launch: 'Have picked up six air crew from dinghy in position so-and-so.'

The launch flashed back only one word: 'Blast!' and turned round and headed for home.

Just one other point strikes me about this rescue incident. It had a fine international flavour.

The British crew in the dinghy included one New Zealander. They were located by Lockheed Hudson aircraft built in California. And they were picked up by a flying-boat manned entirely by Australians. There seems to be a nice touch of co-operation about that.

22. COLOGNE – IN DAYLIGHT

SIX SQUADRONS OF BLENHEIMS OF BOMBER
COMMAND PENETRATED INTO THE RHINELAND THIS
MORNING TO ATTACK THE GREAT COLOGNE POWER
STATIONS AT QUADRATH AND KNAPSACK. FIGHTERS
ACCOMPANIED THE BOMBERS AS FAR AS ANTWERP.
THE BOMBERS WENT ON ALONE, OFTEN FLYING AT
LESS THAN 100 FEET, ON THEIR 150 MILES
PENETRATION OF THE GERMAN DEFENCE SYSTEM.
BOTH POWER STATIONS WERE ATTACKED AT 11.30 A.M.
AT POINT-BLANK RANGE. A GREAT NUMBER OF BOMBS
SCORED DIRECT HITS AND THE TARGETS WERE LEFT
IN FLAMES. (Air Ministry Communiqué)

You may remember in the film 'Target for To-night' a young airman goes around telling the crews where he thinks they're going. When asked how he could possibly know, he says, 'I get around. I get the Gen.' Two days before we attacked the power-house near Cologne, everybody on our station was getting around, getting the 'Gen.' We knew there was something big in the air, but no one was quite certain what it was. In fact, no one had the faintest idea.

We were keyed up when we went into the briefing-room at 6.45 on the morning of the raid, and the Station Commander's opening remarks did nothing to lessen the tension. He started off by saying, 'You are going on the biggest and most ambitious operation ever undertaken by the R.A.F.' Then he told us what it was. Cologne, in daylight. One hundred and fifty odd miles across Germany at tree-top height and then – the power-house. We were given the course to follow, the rendezvous with other squadrons of bombers, and the rendezvous with fighters. We were given the parting point for the fighters and the moment at which certain flights would peel off the formation for the attack on the second power-house, and then – in formation across Germany. Our orders were to destroy our objectives at all costs.

While pilots and observers were getting all they could from the weather man, we rear gunners gathered round the signals officer for identification signs and then hurried out to get ready. Someone said, 'What a trip!' and got the answer, 'Yes, but what a target!'

Knapsack, we were told, was the biggest steam power plant in Europe, producing hundreds of thousands of kilowatts to supply a vital industrial area. If we got it, it would be as good as getting hold of a dozen large factories.

One of the pilots on the raid was in civil life a mains engineer for the County of London Electricity Supply. He came away rubbing his hands and explained to us that, with turbines setting up about 3,000 revolutions a minute, blades were likely to fly off in all directions at astronomical speeds, smashing everything and everyone as they went.

We crossed a fairly choppy sea to the mouth of the Scheldt, flying in probably the biggest formation of bombers ever to deliver a low-level attack. It was grand to see them. Even while we were attacking we knew that other bombers and squadrons of fighters were penetrating deep into the Pas de Calais.

Over Holland we saw fields planted out in the pattern of the Dutch flag. People everywhere waved us on, there was a remarkable amount of red, white and blue washing about the place. I saw one Storm Trooper standing over a group of workers, and when he saw us he ran like a weasel. Near the frontier they did not wave, they just watched us. In Germany itself men scuttled off for shelters. During the whole of our trip we saw no motor transport of any kind.

I was sitting in the rear turret and I didn't know we were over the target until I saw the power-house chimneys above me – four on one side, eight on the other. Then the observer called out, 'Bombs gone,' and as I felt the doors swinging to, the pilot yelled, 'Machine gun!' I burst in all I could as we turned away to starboard. Three miles off I had a good view of the place. We had used delayed-action bombs, and banks of black smoke and scalding steam were gushing out. Debris was rocketing into the air, and I thought of those turbine blades ricocheting around the building.

On the way back we kept sufficiently good formation to worry attacking Me. 109's. The first I knew of them was the leading air-gunner calling out: 'Tally-ho! Tally-ho! Snappers to port beam. Up five hundred.' The attack went on for eight minutes until they broke off and another formation of twelve enemy snappers came into action. They left us when they saw our own chaps coming out to meet us.

Some odd things happened on this raid. One draughty hole in a front perspex was stopped by the gallant observer sticking his seat in it to keep out the gale. Over Holland we flew into hosts of seagulls, and some aircraft brought back specimens stuck in their engine cowling, so giving rise to the suggested Dutch communiqué, 'And from these operations five of our seagulls failed to return.' Twelve ducks also failed to return; one of our aircraft came back with them inside it, all of them dead. But I should think the oddest things of all must have happened inside that power-house at Knapsack.

When we got back we astonished a few people on our station when we told them where we had been. Sometimes we get around too. We also get the 'Gen,' and we certainly got the target.

23. TORPEDO-BOMBER GETS HOME

BEAUFORT AIRCRAFT OF COASTAL COMMAND,
CONTINUING THE HUNT FOR ENEMY SHIPPING OFF
THE SOUTH-WEST COAST OF NORWAY TO-DAY,
LOCATED A GERMAN CONVOY AND TORPEDOED A
SUPPLY VESSEL. (Air Ministry Bulletin)

I'm from the Isle of Man. My observer – we call him 'Daddy' because he is twenty-eight and a year older than I am – comes from Beckenham in Kent, the rear gunner from Camberwell, and the wireless operator from Streatham. Both of these boys are in hospital wounded at the moment, but I hope they will soon be back in my aircraft again.

We carry torpedoes on our Beauforts, and the other day we were ordered to attack a convoy of large enemy ships off the coast of Norway. Three aircraft were to go, led by the Squadron Commander. Unfortunately, my aircraft was delayed a little in getting off the ground, and as such operations are worked to the split second, the other two Beauforts went on ahead.

We had about three hundred miles to go before reaching Norway, and before getting there I did everything to catch up with the other two aircraft, but I couldn't – though I ran into evidence of their work. There was a big black pall of smoke on the horizon, just where we knew the convoy to be, and I soon saw it to be a large ship on fire and listing over.

I picked another ship of about 7,000 tons, went in and released my torpedo. At that second Charlie – that's the rear gunner from Camberwell – yelled through the intercom., 'Look out, skipper – Messerschmitts!'

At the same moment I heard the rattle of a German's guns and the pouf of his cannon shell. The Messerschmitt hit us first time, and I saw tracers going past my head. Then the gunner yelled again, 'Another one coming in, skipper.' They hit us again. I heard our guns going all the time. Charlie, very calmly, said, 'I think I got him'; then a second later, 'Here comes another from the beam.' There was a terrific explosion at the back, and the rear guns stopped. 'Daddy,' the observer, crawled back, and a few seconds later came to tell me, 'Charlie's been hit pretty badly.'

All this time I was throwing the aircraft about, but we were then only about 20 feet above the water. All the time the two Messerschmitts were coming in and letting us have everything they'd got from 20 yards. Every time they hit us my Beaufort shuddered, and I had to fight the controls to keep her out of the sea.

Later I found that the rear gunner, who had been unconscious, had come to, and had opened up again. We are certain he got one of the

Messerschmitts. He filled its belly with lead at less than 20 yards, and didn't see anything more of the Jerry.

Then the rear guns stopped again, and I was chased all over the place. There was some inviting cloud, but I couldn't get the aircraft higher than a few feet, we were so badly hit. I thought a thousand times that we must go into the ditch. But I had to laugh when the observer calmly pulled out his watch and announced that the scrap had lasted for nearly twenty minutes.

Our guns began again. I said, 'By God, those boys are all right.' They had dragged themselves up to the guns and were still fighting. Then the one remaining Messerschmitt came round the front of us. He must have thought we were finished, but after one more squirt from our guns he turned away in a hurry. We didn't see him again.

We had to get home then, and we found that we were heading south instead of west, with about three hundred miles to go in a damaged aircraft. We were just skimming the waves. It was raining hard, blowing a gale, and all the perspex – that's the glass – had been shot away.

We were wet and miserable, and there were two men behind badly hurt. I said, 'We'll have to go down in the water,' but then we found that the rear gunner and wireless operator had collapsed and couldn't move.

We were still only just above the sea. So we decided to try to get home, and we took off our Mae Wests to make a bed for Charlie, as he was really hurt.

It took three hours before we made a landfall, and then we were about two hundred miles south of where we should have been. That's how we had been chased.

When I tried to turn the aircraft right, I found that she wouldn't turn, although I managed to coax her to 80 feet. So we turned out to sea again in a wide circle to the left, and lost sight of land.

Anyhow we got home at last. But, on getting ready to land, I saw the undercarriage swinging about in the breeze. So I just prayed and crash-landed. I was amazed that the Beaufort ever got home after all she'd been through.

OVER TO YOU

The legendary days of Dunkirk and the Battle of Britain; the winged victory in North Africa; fighter sweeps over France; bomber sorties to Germany and Italy; night fighting, train-busting, intruder operations; the work of Ferry Command and the training of pilots in Canada; the remorseless harrying of U-boats; the adventures of air crews forced down in ocean or desert – these are the subjects of *Over to You*, a collection of stories chosen from over 900 broadcasts given by R.A.F. officers and airmen between March 1942 and May 1943.

Over to You is a companion volume to an earlier book of broadcasts by the R.A.F., *We Speak from the Air*.

WINGED VICTORY

Winged victory, we pray you, fly
From Hellas to our northern sky
And let your starry aegis fall
On us who, striving, strive for all.

Endow with virtue and sublime
Success the fighters as they climb
To battle. Let their aim be true
Who now are supplicating you.

And sit with those who nightly ride
The storm-winds and the cloud-strewn tide
That rolls and surges, breaks and roars
In tumult over distant shores.

And when your wings have brought us peace
We will escort you home to Greece,
And set you high where you will be
Man's pilgrimage, sweet Victory.

'Ariel'

This poem is taken from *Winged Victory*, by 'Ariel,' by permission
of Basil Blackwell and Mott, Ltd., Oxford.

CONTENTS

I
THE FATEFUL SUMMER

'The lesson is, never to give in, never, never, never. Not in any event, great or small.'
Winston Churchill

1. DOG-FIGHTS OVER DUNKIRK

The days of Dunkirk when France finally capitulated are far behind, but some of those battles, high up in the sky, have left vivid memories in the minds of many pilots.

I can remember the glorious spring evenings when the sun was going down, lighting the evening with a deep red glow, and our squadron pilots stood outside the dispersal huts, still in full flying kit, waiting for the release from readiness which came only with the darkness.

We stood there at nights watching the endless stream of heavy bombers droning south-eastwards over our heads; the ground crews who stayed by to check our machines after dark, ready for the next day, were counting the heavy chaps as they went out, and a throaty cheer went up as the hundredth ploughed majestically on its way, becoming even smaller until it was lost to sight in the darkness of the east.

Donald and Ralph, my two friends, were beside me – we were a little apart from the rest and Ralph spoke: 'Things are pretty grim over there; I wonder when our turn will come?'

'Old boy, don't you worry,' replied Donald. 'We'll be in the thick of it in the next fortnight; the French will never hold out, and we will have to fight like hell to stop the darned Huns from walking into London.'

They started arguing. For once I was quiet – a little bewildered that so much beauty could come from so grim a setting – and rather amazed at the sudden turn of events on the Continent. War up to now had been just one terrific thrill, but now it was looming up into a threat against Britain, which appeared likely to end in complete and utter disaster.

It was dark and the telephone rang, but instead of the expected release from readiness we were ordered to eat our supper as soon as possible and to arrange for six pilots to be at readiness throughout the night. I was second off the ground that night, so I rolled up in my flying clothes and tried to get some sleep in case I was ordered off later on.

It was after midnight when someone shook me. I jumped up off the bed and started rushing towards the door still only half awake. 'Steady, steady,' a voice said. It was my Commanding Officer. 'You are not wanted to fly, but we have got to go south to be at 'M' by first light, and you will be one of the squadron so get everything ready for 3 o'clock – dawn is at 3.30.'

'What's the matter, sir? Are we going to France?' I asked. 'No,' came the quiet reply. 'The army is evacuating from France. It has started already, and we are going to cover the withdrawal.'

I tried to snatch some more sleep but it was useless. All the time through my mind rushed those few words – 'the army is evacuating.' I was relieved when at last it was time to go out to our aircraft.

It was just growing light. Our Spitfires were standing looking slim and eager to get into the air. There was no wind; a white mist was drifting over the Fens and it was rather chilly and damp.

In this war, by far my most vivid memories are not those of fierce fighting, of firing guns or aeroplanes – they are of quiet moments at the beginning and end of each day when dawn is breaking or night falls. Some of the sunrises that I have seen (and one sees many as a fighter pilot) have been among the most beautiful moments that I can remember.

This was such a morning, everywhere cold, still, and grey; no noise except the hollow-sounding voices of the airmen. Here and there a farm chimney was starting to puff out white smoke as we taxied out in the half-light with our red and green navigation lights burning.

At last we were airborne, packed in tight formation, the long streaks of flame from the exhausts showing up against the dark ground below. Already in the east the sun was rising over the North Sea, tinting everything a dull red. It was all so strangely beautiful, and yet, ever present, was the thought of the grim and dangerous work soon to be done.

We reached 'M,' as ordered, by first light, and as we landed, two other squadrons appeared from the north, circled, and came in. Hot tea and biscuits were passed round by some airmen from the back of a lorry. Within half an hour two more squadrons had landed, and the boundary of the aerodrome was covered in aircraft.

At last we got our instructions. We were to take off as a wing of five squadrons and to patrol the areas south-east of Dunkirk from 05.45 to 06.30 hours. If we used up our ammunition we were to return at once.

We were quiet, then, wondering what it would be like. Fellows tightened revolvers round their waists, ready to fight on the ground if we were shot down.

In an incredibly short time we were airborne. Our job was to patrol at 20,000 feet to stop the German Messerschmitt fighters from protecting their bombers below. Underneath us, three squadrons of Hurricanes were to deal with the bombers. Above us, another squadron of Spitfires patrolled.

We flew straight into the sun on the way over, and I could see very little as my eyes watered with the strain of looking for the enemy. We passed Dunkirk – a huge column of black smoke rising straight up to 15,000 feet hardly moving in the still morning. For thirty-five minutes we flew round inside France when suddenly we saw black dots a little to the north-east of us. We rushed towards them and, in a moment, the sky was full of whirling aircraft, diving, twisting, and turning. Too late, both squadrons realised that we were friends, and although we had not opened fire at one another, it was going to be almost impossible to form up again in our own squadrons.

Round and round we went looking for our sections. I noticed queer little straight lines of smoke very close together as I flew past them. Suddenly I woke up. 'Someone is shooting; it's smoke from incendiary bullets,' I told myself. I gave up all thought of trying to find the rest of the squadron and started searching all round. The French Curtis flying across my front: I went closer to have a look at them. Wow! They weren't Frenchmen, they were Huns – Me. 109s. They turned towards me, and I went into a steep climbing turn. Up the two of them went. Gosh! How they could climb! They were level with me about 400 yards away; another one joined them. I could see no other aeroplanes by now – just the three 109s.

It was a question of who could get the most height first. I opened the throttle as far as it would go. I was gaining a little now, and with my more manoeuvrable Spitfire I could turn inside the 109s. Slowly, in giant spirals, we gained height and, suddenly, I found myself up sun of all three of them. I quickly turned the other way, and they lost me.

Round I came at 26,000 feet, and I was right behind the last 109 – too far away to shoot yet. I gained – oh, so slowly! – but, sure enough, I was gaining. How long could I wait before firing or before the leader saw me? He was weaving about pretty violently now looking for me. At last, I was in range. I pressed the button, and my whole aeroplane shuddered as the eight guns fired. Nothing happened. The 109 flew on. Then, suddenly, there was a flash, and the enemy aircraft flicked over: his port aileron had been hit and had come off. He jettisoned his hood to jump out, and I turned quickly to get another shot when showers of tracer bullets flew past me. I had forgotten the other two 109s.

I flicked over into a quick turn and lost them. It was getting late, and I had not much petrol, I knew, so I dived for home. My Spitfire was gaining speed rapidly. I was away from them, and it was nearly 6.35. How quickly time had gone! The aircraft was going so fast I had to push hard on the stick to keep it in its dive. I started to look round and saw the coast of Dunkirk. Then there came the roar of machine-gun fire. I pulled back on the stick and went up, up, higher and higher, into a huge climbing turn. I could not see what had been firing at me. Anyway, I'd shaken him off, it seemed.

Nose down for home again. I was getting short of petrol; no time for dog-fights now. Faster and faster, and then, again, a burst of machine guns above the roar of the engine. I whirled round into another turn, and as I did so the noise stopped. Then it dawned on me. Fool that I was, it was my own guns firing. As the Spitfire increased its speed in the dive my grip on the stick tightened, and my thumb was still on the firing button after my fight! All the time that I had been taking such violent evasive action, wheeling round the sky, there had been nobody near me. I felt rather stupid dodging round the sky trying to get away from no one at all.

I settled down and got a grip of myself and crossed the Channel at 500 feet. It was an amazing sight, with hundreds of vessels of all sorts of shapes and sizes ploughing backwards and forwards across the Straits. I felt proud of my country, even if we were being forced to leave France. It was incredible to see little 15-ft. motor-boats sailing steadily across towards Dunkirk, unarmed, to face the fury and strength of the Huns.

I have often heard someone described as being a victorious loser. Only now did I realise the true meaning of that expression. Watching these gallant men beneath, one felt an almost irrepressible desire to land on the beach at Margate and to climb aboard one of the boats to share their dangers.

I crossed the English coast at Ramsgate, and saw beneath me the old civilian aerodrome that we had used for our summer camp eighteen months before. How different it looked in its war paint; my mind wandered, dreaming back to the days we had spent in peace time.

Suddenly, a row of white puffs of smoke appeared half a mile ahead of me. It was our own anti-aircraft fire. I had a little ammunition left, and I flew towards it looking everywhere for an enemy aircraft. I sighted nothing until, looming up in the haze which was hanging over the Thames, I saw barrage balloons. I was right in the middle of them so I climbed quickly above them. I still do not know whether the anti-aircraft battery fired to frighten me away from the balloons or whether there really was a German raider. But I stopped my day-dreaming and paid attention to getting home.

By this time I had used so much petrol that I was getting worried about being able to reach base as we had been ordered to do. Slowly the familiar landmarks went by beneath me. Every moment I pressed the petrol gauge. At last, my aerodrome came in sight.

I landed just as another of the squadron was touching down. It was Barrie; we were the only two back so far. We taxied rather quickly, racing to get in first and to tell the story, for there was a crowd waiting on the tarmac. Two hundred yards short of the dispersal point, Barrie ran out of petrol and stopped, so I won the race home.

By ten o'clock three more pilots had returned, making five in all, and we sat down to a terrific breakfast of bacon and eggs and champagne (the chef had produced the champagne). One by one, the pilots came back; practically everyone had shot something down, and many had been damaged slightly. Kenny had the whole of one side of his aeroplane blown out, but he got it home with only a single strand of wire working the controls. 'Sneezy,' while chasing a Messerschmitt 109, had in turn been attacked by four more, and had led a follow-my-leader race down the main street at Dunkirk, only shaking them off by diving between a gasometer and a crane.

There were only two pilots missing, and our squadron score was 10 destroyed, 3 probables, and 3 damaged. By 4 o'clock, it was known that the two missing pilots had not got back to this country. They were Donald and Ralph, my two friends.

We never heard of them again.

2. 'LET US REMEMBER THEM':
BATTLE OF BRITAIN, 1940

A Wing Commander speaks:

It is really very hard to recapture the feeling that I had in the Battle of Britain. In the years that have passed so much has happened.

In those days the only time we saw the pilots of other squadrons was at night after long hours at readiness, when we met in the bar for a quick one. So often just as one was becoming friendly with a pilot he would get shot down, and we would see him no more. Our Air Force term was, and still is, that So-and-so had 'bought it.' Meaning that he was dead, or at the best lying wounded in some hospital.

When we met the Hun we mixed it good and proper; we generally waited for a moment or two until we were in the most favourable position before making the first attack. After the first attack it was every man for himself. There were nearly always many more Huns than ourselves. We whirled around, taking squirts at as many machines as possible; sometimes when they burst into flames the crew baled out or we were lucky enough to see where they hit the ground; then we were able to claim victories.

After the battle we would rush back to the drome, tell our stories to the Intelligence Officer, tell him to buck up and get through to the hospitals to find out if So-and-so had got any confirmed before he was shot down, and ask him to try and salvage something from the Hun wrecks.

Often at the height of the blitz, when we returned we could not remember what on earth had happened, not even what we had fired our guns at; one of the pilots in my Flight, fighting nine Messerschmitt 109s, swore that he had only fired his guns for a one-second burst, yet he had actually finished his ammunition, sixteen seconds' worth.

I do remember clearly seeing the Hun bombers, flying in tight mass formation, crossing the English coast, and thinking to myself that they were about to drop their bombs on my country, my friends, perhaps even my mother, and that I was in a Hurricane and that with God's will I could stop them. I dived to attack and laughed as they broke formation; the crew of a Heinkel baled out; the others turned and ran, spraying me with tracer. Five bullet holes in my plane that time. Within the hour the ground crews had fixed it, and my plane was ready for action.

We always had a devil-may-care sort of happiness. Lying in the sun waiting at readiness, there were moments of great beauty; the colours in the fields seemed brightest and the sky the deepest blue just before taking off for a big blitz. At dusk everything became peaceful. We were all happy at the thought of another day accomplished, our Hurricanes standing silhouetted against the sky, looking strong and confident, the darkness hiding their patched-up paintwork. In the morning whilst it was still dark, the roar of the engines being tested woke us for another day's work.

A Squadron Leader speaks:

A long time has passed since the Battle of Britain, and yet it seems only yesterday that we all crowded round the radiogram in the mess on the night of 15th September, and listened to the scores of the day's fighting – 185 German aircraft destroyed, only 27 of ours missing.

When the Battle of Britain began, I was stationed in the Midlands: our squadron was fresh and ready to go and have a crack at the Huns as they raided Dover and our Channel convoys, but days went by and we began to despair, feeling that we were to be left out of the show. A few squadrons began to come north out of the front line – I remember so well wondering when I heard that a certain squadron was coming north and when only eight aeroplanes landed instead of eighteen – wondering at the grey, tired-faced pilots that came into the mess. But soon I was to know. At last our chance came. On a hot September morning Operations rang – 'Squadron to go to F. at once.'

Then at our new station the first time over the loud speaker, 'Squadrons Scramble London 20,000 ft.'

It all came so quickly. One instant I was asleep on the grass by my aeroplane; a short moment while fumbling fingers strapped me in my Spitfire – my inside felt cold and seemed to be turning over – then bumping across the aerodrome in formation. I do not know what happened after that until a queer artificial voice came over the radio, 'Two hundred bandits crossing Dover flying north at 20,000 feet; some more very high up.' The sky was empty, and everything below us seemed still as if the world was asleep.

Then suddenly we saw them, a huge great rectangle of black bombers, ack-ack bursting all round them, and we were diving towards them. I remember a 110 flying across my nose so close that I saw the pilot looking at me. There were aircraft all round – bombers falling out of formation, black dots of fighters climbing and diving. Away on the left a long black trail of smoke and a blazing red dot going straight down. Then it was all over, and I was back at the aerodrome. Excited pilots were recounting their experiences. I only realised then that I had fired my guns. I felt that it had been a good day – little did I know that twice more that day I would climb up over London, fight, and come home again.

As the days went by it became easier. I grew accustomed to the rush and tumble of a dog-fight, and I had time to think and remember.

They were wonderful, weird, exciting days. Days when aircraft left beautiful curving vapour trails high in the sky, days when some of our friends took off and never came back, when others came back maimed and burnt, never to fight again. Days when the Germans at their bases back in France must have sat and wondered, when their High Command must have been appalled at their growing losses, until at long last into the bullying German mind there came the realisation that they had lost their first battle – the Battle of Britain.

A Flight Lieutenant speaks:

If there is any special significance in that we are the three representing to-day those pilots who lived, and fought, and all too often died, in the skies over Britain two years ago, it is, I think, this:

The two officers whom you have just heard are a walking proof that it is possible to fight this war in the air with distinction, and to come through unscathed; unscathed, but more mature and with an experience invaluable to those who now follow them. I on the other hand, I suppose, speak for those who did not come through unscathed, for those whom it was inevitable that we should lose in that great clash in the heavens before the invader was finally beaten off; for those who, though broken in body, remained unbroken in spirit, and who after a shorter or longer time licking their wounds, are now waiting and eager to fight again.

I was not in the sky on that great day of 15th September. I was in hospital, already asking that first inevitable question of every crashed pilot – 'When do I go back?' Well, it is now two years, and though I am still not back, I know that I have very little longer to wait.

In two years one has learnt a little patience, a little wisdom, and one has learnt to know one's limitations. In those days it was gloriously good sport; this time it will be a job – a hard, tiring job that must be done. Then we fought with our emotions: now it must be with our reason. We who have now been out of the battle for two years know the other side of the picture, and it is not pleasant; but go on we must – there can be no turning back.

Thinking now of those days, I find that what remains most clearly in my memory is not the sweating strain of the actual fighting, not the hurried meals, the creeping from bed at dawn, not even the loss of one's friends; but rather those odd stolen moments of peace in the middle of all the pandemonium – the heat haze lying lazily over the airfield while we sat munching a piece of grass, waiting to take off; that curiously lovely moment of twilight after the last Spitfire had landed, after the last engine had been switched off, and before the first night fighter took the air, the first searchlight split the darkness and the first wail of the siren was heard again – that moment when the evening lay spread out against the sky, giving for an instant a mocking glimpse of stillness and peace before night fell suddenly like a curtain and the whole hideous cacophony of war broke out afresh. But, above all, the thing that remains most clearly imprinted on my memory is the spirit which then existed – the same spirit which inspired everybody from the Station Commander to the lowest aircraft-hand. A spirit no better than that which now exists, but one which to us who then fought must seem different and rather special. For that was the first trial, the first flush of battle, and it was a great hour.

II
FIGHTERS UP!

'But when my gunning beauty
Spurts cloudward for its duty,
I am one of the zenith's earls
And the stars' crusader.'
Lord Derwent

1. DAWN PATROL

I'm not good at getting up early – really early, I mean – and even in summer the early-morning air at 4 a.m. is chilly. But it has its compensations, for after you've overcome the revulsion of getting out of a warm bed, there's something exhilarating and thrilling at that hour of the morning, especially when there's the prospect of a flying trip ahead. As a rule it's a good thing to have a cup of tea or something hot and a biscuit. It helps a lot towards waking you up.

When we get to the aerodrome it's still quite dark, except for the crescent of the last quarter of the moon and a very faint tinge of light in the east. The Met. forecast shows that we're lucky, and it's clearly going to be a fine day. A gentle breeze of ten miles an hour from the south, three-tenths to five-tenths cloud at five thousand feet, and a visibility of twelve miles or more. The Bomber boys were out last night, and a distress signal has been received saying that someone was down in the ditch 30 miles north-east of Calais. The boats are out searching, and I hope we shall have a chance of looking for them when we get out there.

Although it's still too dark to take off, we can just make out the faint silhouette of aircraft parked by the perimeter track. They look rather ghostly, and yet somewhat animal with their long snouts; the thick cable from the engine to the battery starter trolley – that's a large box containing an accumulator – gives them the appearance of being tethered to a trough.

As we arrive at the Flight Dispersal, one engine after another starts with a roar. My aircraft has already been warmed up and is ready for me to climb and take off. In the dark you may see a few sparks, but otherwise all you can detect is a faint mauve halo along a line of red-hot exhaust pipes.

As I get on to the wing of my aircraft, I notice that the morning dew and condensation have caused the windscreen and perspex hood to mist up; that's inevitable, but it will clear up as soon as we reach the cold air above.

Then I'm airborne. Although the Duty Pilot has seen me take off and will phone the information to Group Headquarters, I must book-in by wireless, so as soon as I'm in the air I press the 'Transmit' switch on my R/T set. 'Hallo, Bolton Control, Bolton Control. Party 24 airborne. Over.' It's always a good thing to keep messages short, as it does not then give the Hun any time to plot my position. Immediately back comes the reply, 'Hallo, Party 24, 24, Bolton Control answering. Receiving you loud and clear. I have no information for you. Listening out.' That means that no enemy aircraft are reported in my vicinity, that Group know they can get into touch with me if and when they want to, and also confirms that my transmission is satisfactory.

Let's decide to climb above this first cloud layer and steer on 270 degrees. As the altimeter marks 4,000 feet, we get our first glimpse of the sun. At present it's just a red ball partially concealed by small clouds; the channel and land below me are still in shadow, but the lights and changing colours reflected on the clouds must be seen to be believed. I wish I were an artist and could paint them; I always feel that a sunrise seen from the air is so beautiful that, were an artist to paint one truthfully, he would be accused of exaggeration. I wonder why it is so much more beautiful from the air than from ground level?

We are now passing through the light cloud layer. Small white wisps rush past me and the ground is blotted out as I break surface on top. It's glorious up here. The engine thrusts forward with a powerful roar, and although I'm in one of the fastest and deadliest of warplanes, I feel miles away from the war and rather tempted to day-dream. But that must stop right away. My position, silhouetted against the patch of white cloud, makes me vulnerable, for I can be seen very easily if there are any Huns above me. I take a good look around the sky, paying particular attention to that area behind me. There's nothing about, so we continue to climb towards the south-east. At 10,000 feet, I level out and take notes of the weather. The height, formation and amount of cloud, the temperature and visibility. All this I jot down on the writing-pad strapped to my knee. Below me the clouds have thinned out, and I am now immediately above a Belgian coast town which was formerly a well-known holiday resort. I note any ships I can see, and then turn through 180 degrees to dive down through the fast-disappearing cloud. To my right we can see the long white wake of an air-sea rescue launch. It must be searching for the bomber crew reported during the night. We shall not be able to spare much time looking for them, and there will be plenty or other aircraft doing that job, but – you never know – we might be lucky. I open the hood above my cockpit, for two reasons. It's easier to search by leaning a little out of the cockpit, and also I have a horror of falling into the water and being trapped inside. Higher up, I always fly with the hood closed, because I would have ample time to jettison if my engine failed or if I were unfortunate enough to be shot down. Low down I might not have the time before my aircraft hit the water and, you know, Spitfires don't float.

There's quite a lot of wreckage and oil floating about in the Channel these days, which makes me turn back several times and circle over a piece of wood or oil patch, fearing I might miss something or somebody. Every now and again I glance in the mirror above the windscreen or look behind me in case an enemy aircraft has spotted me and is creeping up. There doesn't seem to be anything about, so I think I – what's that? What a lucky break! Right below me, a large bomber's dinghy with five chaps in it. The sea all round is coloured bright green from the fluorescein carried in the Mae Wests, which helps so much to attract the attention of searching aircraft. Climbing above my 'find,' I circle and carefully note the position of the nearest rescue launch some six miles away. The rest is easy. I attract the attention of the launch and send it in the direction of the dinghy. They acknowledge my signals, and in a few minutes I know the bomber crew will be picked up.

We've now been airborne 40 minutes. Allowing, say, 20 minutes' scrapping, in case we meet anything in the air, that will leave about 30 minutes in which to play around. I decide to go and see if there's anything interesting inside France. We'll go down to nought feet and cross the coast between Boulogne and Calais. The cliffs at this part of the French coast are very like the ones at Dover, and on one occasion, I remember, I thought they were the English ones. We had been engaged somewhere in the middle of the Channel and I had got rid of a Hun off my tail by spinning down, and I turned to the right and headed south instead of north. I soon found out my mistake, because it seemed as if every anti-aircraft gun in France was having a pot at me, and I can't tell you to this day why I wasn't hit. However, that's another story.

Here's the coast. Now ease the stick gently back to scrape over the top of the cliffs, and we're over France. There doesn't seem to be any sign of life at this hour of the morning (it's just 5.45); but that doesn't mean much, and I'm quite sure that we've been spotted by some defence post; but we are too low and moving too quickly for anyone to have a shot at us. Trees and isolated houses flash by as we streak along at nearly 300 miles an hour. I'm looking for the aerodrome just south of the town we've passed, but it's impossible to read a map at this speed and, anyway, I want both eyes to watch the ground ahead and to avoid trees and other obstacles which appear as if from nowhere under my wings.

A clump of buildings ahead looks familiar; so also does that line of electric-light pylons to my right. Yes, I can now see the burnt-out remains of a hangar which was set on fire during one of the bombing attacks at the beginning of the summer. It's the aerodrome all right and the people on it are awake, for cutting across my port wing I can see thin white streaks. Flak. I can't hear any sounds of gunfire above the noise of the engine, but catch a glimpse of the gunpost on our left as we pass. Right ahead of me is what I'm really looking for – a couple of aircraft parked in front of a dispersal bay. I haven't the time to make out the type (they are probably 190s or 109s), and as my sight ring covers one of them, I press the gun-firing button on the control column. Small pencils of smoke reach out from each wing as my cannons fire. Although I can hear the guns firing, I'm not so much conscious of the noise they make as of the vibration and momentary drop in speed of the aircraft. It's a sensation hard to describe. Rather like standing very close to one of those pneumatic road drills where the noise is not deafening but seems to go through you and everything seems quiet in comparison when it leaves off.

As I pass a couple of feet above the enemy aircraft, there's a blinding flash of white flame, and a puff of oily black smoke is thrown into the air. Our cannon shells have hit it all right, and I would very much like to stay and watch it burning, but as all the guns round the aerodrome are having a crack at me, I resist the temptation and crouch lower in my seat. Not that crouching any lower would do the slightest bit of good if the aeroplane were hit fair and square, but somehow I feel as if I want to make myself very scarce just now. I keep the aircraft right down on the deck and shave a farmhouse or some building on the far side of the aerodrome, then down a small valley (I wish it were deeper) and hard right at the end of it so as to put as much distance and as many trees and buildings and things as possible between me and those red tracers which seem to follow after me. We haven't been hit, and there doesn't appear to be a single Hun in the sky. Anyway, I've used up a lot of my ammunition, and I feel that I've had my fun for this morning, so we'll just turn through 90 degrees to starboard and head for home.

Half-way across the Channel I pass over the rescue launch with the bomber's dinghy alongside. A couple of the crew wave and give the thumbs-up signal. Good show. They'll be back in England in time for breakfast. And talking of breakfast, am I hungry?

2. 'YOU DON'T MAKE
THE SAME MISTAKE TWICE'

In air fighting a pilot doesn't usually make the same mistake twice. Either he frightens himself so much that he never does it again or else – well, he's unlucky, and that way too he doesn't make the same mistake again. I'm remembering a mistake I made not so very long ago. I think you'll agree that I was lucky.

It was on one of those lovely English summer days on our aerodrome on the south coast. We were standing in our shirt sleeves and Mae Wests by the barbed wire near the dispersal hut. We could see the coast of France faintly on the horizon. Twenty feet away a couple of fitters were crawling over my Spitfire and tinkering with the engine, the aircraft looking slightly undressed with its engine cowlings on the ground beside it. No one had had a scrap for over a week. Nobody had even seen an enemy aircraft in the sky for over a week. I hadn't yet met a Hun in the sky at all. I remember someone saying, 'It's a dull life,' and we all agreed.

Half an hour later the C.O. told me to go and have a look at the weather at 30,000 feet over on the other side. I think Group Headquarters wanted to know whether it was fit to send over a sweep. I was as pleased as Punch. A lovely day. A climb up to 30,000, and I might find my first Hun somewhere over the water. What more could you wish for?

I took off and headed north in order to gain height first, before turning south and flying over France. It's best to cross the French coast either high up or at nought feet; if you go across at a height which is neither one thing nor the other, the Hun usually throws up a lot of dirt. It doesn't often hit you, but it makes things rather uncomfortable. Besides, it gives him plenty of warning.

At 12,000 feet, I could see both sides of the Channel there. The sea was as calm as a mill-pond. Here and there, dotted about the Channel, I could make out rescue buoys; and as I turned round towards France and Belgium, I could see woods and fields stretching for miles inland. It was then, I remember, my radio crackled in my headphones. It was the Controller back at base. He was warning me that there were a few bandits sculling about to the south of me. Well, I acknowledged the message, the warning, and I looked all round the sky, but saw nothing. I continued to climb steadily. Now below me was the balloon barrage over Dover harbour. The balloons looked like grey drawing-pins stuck into the kind of model landscape one used to see at exhibitions. There was no shipping in sight.

At 20,000 feet I levelled out. My engine was running perfectly, and I started to hum a tune. I felt so much on top of the world and wondered what it was about flying on a perfect day which you don't describe but – it gets into your blood and makes you happy. I looked down at Boulogne harbour four miles below me. The sun was very bright and glistened on a small patch of white frost forming on the inside of my perspex hood. By holding up my hand and squinting through my almost-closed fingers, I could just look into the sun, and satisfied myself that there was nothing above me. I was about to look behind me and examine the rest of the sky when I happened to glance down at the chessboard cultivation of France. Then I saw a small black speck moving slowly across the landscape. It might be a bird. The size was right. But it wasn't a bird. It moved too smoothly and regularly for that. It was the one thing I'd always been hoping to meet. I'd never been lucky enough to come across him before. My first Hun and by himself.

Keeping my eye on him all the time (otherwise I should have lost sight of him and might never have picked him up again against the dark background), I turned to the right so that I could dive down from out of the sun and come in from behind him. It was then I heard a crackling over my radio transmitter. It was the Controller again saying something about 'Bandits.' He was warning me; but I was far too excited to listen to him. I just acknowledged the message with a curt 'O.K.' and, turning on the electric light in my gun sight and pushing forward the control column I started to go after my Hun.

The extra speed of my dive made the controls feel hard and stiff. The noise increased, and I could hear the whine of the slipstream as it rushed over my cockpit cover. Slowly I drew closer to my target. Very slowly, it seemed. But when I glanced at my airspeed indicator, I realised that it was 'off the clock' – that meant over 400 miles an hour. Oh – I'd almost forgotten to turn the gun-firing button on the control column from 'Safe' to 'Fire.' So I had the stick in my left hand and turned the knob with my right. Now, I was fairly tearing down. The enemy aircraft was still some distance below me. It began to take the shape of a 109 F. Now I could see the crosses on the wings. I could just make out the double 'V' sign on the long black fuselage. I knew that the pilot couldn't have seen me, as I was coming straight out of the sun. He just continued on a straight course. I was afraid that I was going to overshoot and flash past him without having time to get him in my sights. So very gently I eased back the control column and started to turn in a wide circle to the right. Then I could come up on him directly from behind. I was overtaking him quickly. My eyes were glued to his tail unit, and his wings were spreading wider in my gun sight. His tail unit was now dead in front of me. Now the two cross bars of the sight cut the fuselage behind the pilot's head. I pressed the firing button. Now! I felt the shudder as the guns fired, and saw the flash as the shells of my cannons went home into the aeroplane in front of me. A second later and I had to pull back the stick or I should have collided.

As I climbed almost vertically above and looked back and down over my shoulder, I saw a large mass of flame and black smoke. He could never have known what hit him. His whole machine exploded and disintegrated in the air. I continued to do a gentle turn, watching the flaming wreckage spinning down towards the ground some 15,000 feet below.

And then suddenly my own aircraft seemed to leap forward and shake itself. I felt the thud of the bullets hitting the fuselage behind me. As I looked at my instrument panel, it shattered. One of the instruments fell out, hitting my knee. I wondered vaguely how the shell had hit it without passing through my body. My side windshields splintered and let in a rush of cold air which took my breath away even though my face was covered by my oxygen mask. A large star appeared in the thick bullet-proof windscreen just above my head. Thick smoke and a smell of hot oil started to come up from the floor of the cockpit. I wondered what on earth would be next. You see, I'd just been watching an aircraft explode.

Telling you this takes time, but it actually took place so quickly that I hardly knew what had happened. It took time to realise I'd been shot up from behind, to remember the warning over the radio telephone. But I hadn't even the time to curse myself.

I whipped my machine over on to its back and the blood rushed away from my eyes, blacking me out for a second. The next moment I was diving down towards the ground. I hadn't yet seen what had hit me and automatically glanced up at my mirror to see if there was anyone still on my tail. But the mirror had disappeared, and all that remained was a piece of twisted metal perched ridiculously on top of the bent framework of my windscreen. I banked from side to side and looked behind me. Yes, above me and slightly to my right was an F. W. 190 getting into position for another attack on me.

I had to think quick. My radiator had been holed, that was certain. Besides, I didn't know what other damage there was. If my radiator was leaking, the motor might seize up at any minute. And somehow I had to shake off this Hun. He probably knew that he'd lamed me and was now waiting to finish me off.

I waited until he started to dive towards me. Then once again did a quick flick roll on to my back and dived almost vertically towards the French coast below. It was more uncomfortable, the dive, this time, for my aircraft was vibrating and it was as much as I could do to keep it straight. I guessed the tail had been hit; and probably the rudder was damaged, for I had to keep both feet on the port rudder control to prevent it from yawing to the right. The wind rushed through my splintered windscreen, tearing the oxygen mask from my face and pushing it up over my eyes so that I could hardly see or breathe. The sweat was running down my face and into my mouth, which was as dry as a bone. A few feet above the sea I levelled out and looked behind me. The 190 was nowhere to be seen. Whether I had lost him in the dive or whether he thought that he'd finished me off and I was diving down out of control, I shan't ever know.

With a great sigh of relief, and thinking my troubles were over, I sat back in my cockpit. Only to jump up the next second with my heart in my mouth. My engine cut. There was no time to bale out or give my position to base. Long ago I had discovered that my wireless set had been shot away, and anyway I hadn't got a microphone any more. I braced myself with my elbows against the sides of the cockpit and waited for the crash and the shock of cold water.

Suddenly the engine picked up again and very gingerly I climbed up to 500 feet. Twice more it cut, and twice more it started again. I wasn't quite so frightened the last two times, for I should have had time to bale out and had already loosened my straps and thrown away what remained of my helmet.

At long last the aerodrome appeared below me. I landed, and shakily I climbed out and looked at my aircraft. It was like a colander. How it came back I shall never understand. The fitter and the rigger who came up on the ambulance to meet me – they couldn't get it either.

Well, that adventure taught me a good lesson. Since then I've always listened to what the Controller had to say, and I always take a darn good look behind me before going after Huns. I think my lesson was cheap at the price.

3. ESCORT TO LILLE

Ibelieve that, before Ops, everybody gets that funny feeling in the pit of the tummy. There isn't much outward sign of it, except perhaps a little extra laughter at some of the very weak jokes which are cracked on these occasions.

Let's imagine we're in the dispersal hut waiting to be briefed for a cross-Channel sweep. As soon as the Wing Commander Flying – he's the fellow who leads our wing – enters the hut, all chatter ceases. We're getting accustomed to seeing him each day sit on one of the tables and say, with a smile, 'An easy one to-day, chaps; just a quickie over St. Omer and back via Calais,' or something to that effect. But to-day, as he puts it, it isn't quite such a 'quickie,' as we're flying somewhat farther; the target for the bombers is Lille. The Wing Commander is now reading out to us the particulars of the sweep. We're to take off at two minutes past three, climb up and rendezvous with the rest of the party at three-seventeen over Blank-on-Sea, then fly with the bombers to Lille and stick by them. Good enough. We discuss the order of take-off and the order and position in which we should fly – a most important detail, otherwise everyone might start milling around and the sky would be full of Spitfires looking for each other.

It's exactly a quarter to three when we leave the dispersal hut – just time to finish a cigarette, put on my scarf and Mae West, and saunter out to my aircraft where one of the crew is holding my parachute ready. It's a lovely day, sunny, with a few cumulus clouds a couple of thousand feet up. Mentally, I note that the wind is blowing gently from the south and that visibility is good. As always, my aircraft looks as clean as a new pin. The fitter who is standing on the wing helps me into the cockpit and hands me my helmet and gauntlets and a map. Long ago, I learned that it is essential to be comfortable in an aeroplane, and a Spitfire is small enough to sit in even without all the impedimenta which a fighter pilot has to carry with him on these occasions. I plug in my telephone jack and oxygen tube; then I strap myself in tightly, and put the map in the pocket provided for it. I know that it's quite unnecessary to ask whether the aircraft has been refuelled, the guns loaded, the oxygen bottle charged, or whether the clock synchronised. That has all been automatically carried out. Like every other pilot, I know that I can rely implicitly on my ground staff to see that all this was done as soon as I landed from my last flight.

As I look around the aerodrome, I see other pilots climbing into their aircraft and settling themselves comfortably. Over on the far side of the field one of the other squadrons in our wing is also getting ready to take off; I can see airmen running about. This squadron's due to leave shortly after us and to form up on us as soon as we're airborne. Hello! the Wing Commander's aircraft has burst into life; that's the signal for all of us to start up. I unscrew the doping cock and give a few pumps to richen the mixture in the cylinders. As I press the self-starter button and turn on the magneto switches my airscrew begins to revolve, and some sheets of flame belch out from the exhaust ports; I can feel the heat of them on my face. Suddenly, with a deep roar the engine picks up, and I throttle back until it ticks over regularly. Next, I wave the airmen away from my wing-tips and follow the Wing Commander as he taxies round the side of the field. We jolt over the ground, and just before turning into wind and getting into position for taking off, I press the switch on my R/T set; a few seconds later I hear that familiar wave and faint crackle in my headphones. Then – a few bumps and we're airborne. With my right hand I move the lever to raise the undercarriage, and after pulling back the airscrew pitch control with my left hand, I close the hood over my head. The vacuum caused by shutting myself in momentarily affects my hearing, but I swallow once – that's to equalise the air pressure on the inside of my ears – and then all's well. The green light on the dashboard in front of me vanishes, and in its place a red light appears which indicates that the undercarriage is fully locked in the 'up' position. Now a quick glance around the cockpit to make sure that everything is working properly and then, settling back comfortably in my seat, I start the long climb ahead. But my engine temperature's rather high. Well, it did tick over for a fairly long spell on the ground, so I open the radiator flap to the cool air outside, and I make a mental note that I must close it again when we get higher up, or my engine will cool off too much. Slowly we climb up along the coast. That peculiar feeling inside me has disappeared now and I feel fine and ready for anything. I can see the other Spitfires both on my right and left; their pilots look expressionless and rather grotesque with their faces covered by their oxygen masks.

At 12,000 feet I turn on my oxygen, but apart from noticing the flicker of the needle registering the flow, I can't detect any other sign. Oxygen *as* oxygen isn't noticeable so long as the feed is all right, and there's plenty of it; it's when there's a lack of it one feels uncomfortable. And it doesn't give you any warning either. On one occasion, I remember, I was caught with an oxygen failure at 22,000; at one moment I was flying along quite merrily, but at the next – when I came to – I found myself spinning down to earth with my altimeter marking 5,000 feet.

Well, here we are at 18,000 feet and approaching Blank-on-Sea. I close the radiator flap, and although I'm only wearing a sweater over my shirt and trousers, I feel quite warm with the hood shut. My clock shows that according to schedule we should be sighting the bombers with their escort of Spitfires provided by a neighbouring wing within the next minute or so. There they are approaching from inland; they're quite easily recognisable by their shape, and by the close formation in which they fly. We allow them to pass us, and then we climb above, always keeping them in full view.

Half-way over the Channel we take up our battle positions by increasing the distance between aircraft – that's so that each individual pilot may watch over his friend's tail. At the same time, we keep the bombers in view, and watch the sky all round them. Slowly – it seems slowly, because by now we're high up, but actually our speed is well over 280 miles per hour – we approach the French coast, and cross it near Boulogne. I can see one or two puffs of black cotton wool near the bombers – anti-aircraft fire from the Boulogne defences has started up. As I watch, more and more puffs appear all round us. Above the noise of my engine I can't hear any sound of explosion; the puffs remain quite innocuous until one bursts about 20 feet from my starboard wing and very close to the aircraft on my right. I hear the faint 'crump' and can see the vicious orange centre as it explodes. The aeroplane next to mine rocks slightly. I look round quickly; all's well – the pilot has put his thumb up!

Now the silence has been broken by the Controller back at our base; he tells us that there are enemy aircraft climbing up towards us from the south-east, a message acknowledged from the wing leader by a curt 'O.K.' Hearing voices is always a comfort; these are crystal clear in my headphones. Suddenly from the wing leader, 'There they are – right – three o'clock,' and as I look in that direction, I can just see them as flies in the distance against a white cloud. I try to count them, but at present the specks are still too far away. Anyhow, as they're still below us they won't attack, but they'll maintain their climb into the sun, and choose their own time and position – if they do attack, which isn't at all certain. We're passing over St. Omer and approaching Lille. Although I haven't yet had time to examine the ground, I can already recognise certain landmarks, for I am daily becoming more and more familiar with them. I spot the aerodrome near St. Omer: it's just visible as a small square. Two narrow strips cutting across it are the runways. Just behind me is a large green patch; that would be the Forêt de Nieppe, and immediately below us is the canal which runs from Dunkirk to Bethune.

We're almost on top of Lille now, and the bombers are flying in close formation in front of us. As I look at them, their bombs leave in a shower and flash towards the ground. If only I could follow them down and watch them explode on their target! But I've been on too many of these shows to do that sort of thing, for I know that at any minute we're likely to be attacked by odd Huns who'll dive down and try to break up our formation. All the way from the coast there's been spasmodic ack-ack, but now we're over Lille it's very much thicker. But nobody's hit. The bombers have launched their second salvo of eggs; and they fly through as if there were nothing to hamper them, and start then to turn through 180 degrees.

We turn with them – steeply in order to afford protection if they're attacked at this moment when they're more vulnerable. I squint up continually into the sun because I know that if an attack is made, it'll come from that direction. 'Hello! Clinker Leader, Ratter Blue One here. Two 109s at nine o'clock above. Watch 'em.' I look up to the left. There they are – two black brutes with slightly longer fuselage and blunter wing-tips than ours. I wonder will they dive on to us, or on to the bombers? Neither. Two Spitfires from another squadron above come tearing down; one of them is already firing, for I can see some red tracer coming from his cannon. Good show! One of the 109s reels kind of drunkenly on to his back with white and black smoke pouring out of him. The other? No, the other has done a flick half-roll, and dives down towards the ground; he seems to have got away all right. But the first 109 is now a blazing mass of wreckage leaving a trail of thick black oily smoke behind him.

I can't watch any longer because our own squadron is being threatened, and the wing leader has ordered us to turn to the right – into the attackers. I do a steep turn, holding the stick well into my tummy until a kind of red mist begins to form in front of my eyes. That's a warning that, if I turn any tighter, I shall black out. So, gently, I ease the stick forward and look all around me. I am banked vertically, so I look up instead of to the right where the ground appears to be spinning round. Two more black 109s flash by at terrific speed, and disappear before I get a chance to open fire on them. I let them go, a lesson I've learned since doing these sweeps. Never follow a Hun down. You see, our job is to watch the bombers and prevent them from being attacked. It doesn't matter two hoots if we don't shoot down any enemy aircraft; other squadrons on our flanks and above us are there for that job. So long as the bombers get back safely to their base we shall have done our stuff.

We're straightening up again now. A further warning comes along that two more enemy aircraft are diving towards the bombers. But they don't get very far because a couple of Spitfires detach themselves from the section on my right, turn towards the Huns and head off their attack. As ours open fire, I can see a piece of a 109's tail drop off whilst he turns away in a dive.

Now I can also see small formations of Huns above, and on the flanks of our wing. They don't attack, but now and again they make feints in the hope that some of our fighters will draw off to attack them, and become stragglers. We've had so many warnings of these tactics that nobody buys, and we just stay together. We approach Dunkirk; every moment the ack-ack becomes fiercer and fiercer. It seems quite inconceivable that the bombers can fly through all that dirt and neither get separated nor shot down. One of them is hit, however, and lags behind the rest of the formation. Immediately, six Spitfires leave our wing and stay with him to ward off any attack by enemy aircraft still flying along with us, and waiting for such a victim. But as far as I can see our bomber hasn't been badly hit, and one engine is working. We are in gliding distance of Dover from a height of 20,000 feet, so I'm sure that he'll reach base all right. Those white cliffs are always a welcome sight; I fancy that most fellows must breathe a sigh of relief when they're visible. I know I do.

A few minutes later we're crossing the balloon barrage at Dover; the bombers fly straight on towards their base whilst we turn to the right and make our way home. We're losing height more quickly now, and I regulate my flow of oxygen so that the needle of the gauge coincides with the height marked on my altimeter. Well, although I haven't even fired once, I'm quite pleased with myself; after all, I've done a small job of work. I know all the other pilots feel the same whether they've fired their guns or not, because you see 'all our bombers returned safely.' That's all we really worry about.

4. 'BANDITS BELOW!'

The trip to Europe in daylight has become a normal business nowadays. The one I'm going to tell you about was an ordinary one. In the operations room I was handed the orders to carry out a sweep of the Cherbourg peninsula, from de la Hague to Cap Barfleur, to be precise. It was for two o'clock in the afternoon – a time we like, because it gives us a chance for a decent lunch. Taking off is such a routine business that it's as difficult to describe as the way you get dressed in the morning. It's when I shout, 'All clear! Contact!' and the engine bursts into life that I get a fresh feeling, a mixture between excitement and interest, and see the rest of the squadron I'm leading taxi into take-off position. As we cross the coast of England I glance up at the other two squadrons overhead. They look like a school of fish swimming through a deep blue sea, and below us is the real sea. It seems to be all around us, and some days I've had a queer little panicky sensation that I'd drop into it and be drowned. But soon a dark line forms on the horizon. It's the French coast, and in front of it the Channel Islands. On Guernsey the sun catches some of the many glasshouses and turns them into glinting fragments of light. While you see all this with one part of your mind, you're aware of the war with another. Behind, the formation is loosening up. The weavers, who turn and twist to keep a constant look-out behind, are darting from one side of the formation to the other.

We are over the coast now. Below and behind are a few bursts of flak. I peer suspiciously into the sky, towards the sun, but before I've seen anything anywhere one of the weavers starts talking over the R/T. 'Three bandits three o'clock below,' he says. I look down to my right. 'O.K.' I reply, 'bandits sighted, turning right, going down.' We dive. I try to get my sights on one of them, but I'm too far away. A couple dive steeply away to the south and are followed by Spitfires. The other is right in the middle of the top squadron now, and I watch the guns firing from a Spitfire's wing, black smoke streaming from them. I come up from underneath and open fire from about 150 yards. Someone else is firing from very close range on his tail. Little flashes of light leap from his belly. One or both of us are hitting him. Then a burst of grey smoke and a trail of white, meaning he is hit in the oil and radiator. He hangs in the air for a second, then drops, spinning, trailing smoke. I watch him as a Spitfire follows him down.

I steady our chaps up, and set course again. I start counting, and find we're still all there. Then a voice on the R/T again: 'Nine bandits, nine o'clock above.'

They're well above us going south. I keep my eye on them and watch the sun. But as often happens they're not in a playful mood. They go on to the south and we don't give chase because they've got the advantage of height and they may be decoys enticing us to a group of friends farther inland. Over Cherbourg harbour the only shipping to be seen is a small boat in the inner harbour. We search the skies, but there's nothing there. Now Barfleur is to the north of us, and so we start a gentle turn on our homeward course. France, looking completely at peace, fades away; in the interval while we are out of sight of land we gradually lose height, with the weavers still dark across the formation. The English coast begins to take shape – the Isle of Wight and, far to the west, Portland Bill. In a few minutes the squadrons break away and the aircraft spread out and hurry in to land. This time there had been no casualties on our side. But on theirs there were three very frightened Huns, one probably killed, two damaged planes, one probably destroyed, and nine other scared German pilots.

5. 'THE MORAL IS – KEEP WEAVING'

Many times you have heard on the news that the R.A.F. have been over Northern France, that (shall we take as an example?) the docks of Le Havre were bombed, and sometimes the cheering sentence, 'None of our aircraft are missing.' I am going to try and describe what happened on one of those parties to Le Havre that took place recently.

The Wing that I led consisted of three squadrons, very good squadrons too. Though to hear them talk you would think that they were waiting to enter the tower of Babel. I was proud to have a representative of pilots from nearly all our allies. Sometimes when we were driving to our aircraft in a large bus, the boys would start singing: when they did that, I knew that everything would be all right.

The job we had to do that day was to act as rear support to twelve Boston bombers, who of course had another Wing as close escort. As rear support it was our responsibility to cover the homeward journey of the main formation. The time came for us to clamber in the cockpits, taxi out, and take off. The formation soon formed up and we set course. It's a grand feeling to lead a sweep. You look round and see if everyone is in good position. On the right Bobby in M for Mother made rude signs with his fingers, Bertie over on the left gave a thumbs-up, which I returned. Everything is O.K.

England faded in the haze behind. Below us and all around was the sea. Even that had something to cheer us that day, for one of our Air-Sea Rescue boats was skimming along, leaving a lovely white wake. As yet I haven't fallen in the drink; but it's a very comforting feeling knowing those Air-Sea Rescue boys are waiting for you if you do. In less than a minute the boat had disappeared. After a time I peered forward; almost as a shock I saw the French coast. I was about a mile too far east, and about 30 seconds early. Up to now we had been flying in silence, but now one of the weavers – they are our look-outs – had seen the other formation. 'Hullo, Leader, Blue 2 calling, our friends are in front below.' Thank heaven for that, I thought. I turned gently and saw them. The bombers flying in four groups of tight vic formation, surrounded by waltzing Spitfires, dancing around, their wings glinting in the sun.

We were some way above them. I swung the formation out to one side, up sun, because the Hun will be there if he is going to attack. We crossed the coast. Sandhills, then green fields, slid under my wing. I stared at the sun, wondering. Around the bomber formation sprouted mushrooms of dirty black smoke. Flak. A few optimistic gunners had a crack at us; just a bit too far behind, thank you. It's on these shows that one gets such terrific admiration for those bomber boys; they just sail on, dead straight, dead level, making their bombing run, whilst all the time they are a kind of Aunt

Sally for the Hun gunners. Bombs gone. You could see them leave the aircraft, black dots sailing down together, disappearing in the haze; then a long wait, it seemed an age, before on the ground dirty splodges billowed upwards. It was damned good shooting. The docks were hit fair and square; a large ship seemed to have two direct hits, and some oil tanks went up with a whouf of flame. A column of black smoke rose lazily upwards. The sky above was still an unbroken blue. Where are the Huns? Now for home. The bombers wheeled beneath us heading for the sea. Flak still burst round them. All twelve were still in the formation.

Once more we were over the sea, heading for home. I screwed my neck round and stared at the sun. Are those liver spots? 'Hallo, Leader, Red 2 calling, Bandits behind and above us.' Evidently not liver spots. 'O.K., boys,' I replied, 'keep your eyes on them and let me know if they get any closer.' The bomber formation was dead in front below. It's amazing how, when you are being chased by Huns, you feel as if you are going about three miles per hour. Another voice on the wireless, 'There are about forty Huns now, still above.' 'Stick together, chaps,' I replied, 'We'll turn and fight in a minute or two.' I could see the Huns clearly, riding high above us. Suddenly there was a babel of voices, all talking at once, 'Oh, oh, here they come.'

We whipped into a steep turn to meet them; they were firing as they dived. All around me Spitfires started firing too. I gave a quick burst at a Hun that was climbing dead in front of me, then turned round again to catch up with the bombers. The Huns seemed cautious; they didn't try another attack. I stopped weaving and straightened up so that the formation could get together again. Still below and in front the bombers sailed on unperturbed. Suddenly on the wireless came, '*Look out, look out*, Leader!' Quick, that's me. I woke up with a jump, pulled the stick hard back into my tummy and zoomed into a climbing turn. Just in time. Behind me, rolling on to its back, was a Focke-Wulf 190, which had been having a very good crack at me. It dived vertically with two Spitfires hard after it. Black smoke trailing from their wings showed me that they were having a good squirt. After that, I decided that my boys could formate on me whilst I did a little weaving.

At last England jumped out of the haze at us. When we landed we found that we were all back. Two of our planes were damaged by bullets – to my surprise, not mine; ten of us had fired our guns; between us we claimed one Hun destroyed and four damaged. We had a good party that night. The moral for fighter pilots is – keep weaving.

6. FOUR IN A NIGHT

The curious thing about the first one I shot down was that although London was throwing up a terrific amount of flak and there were any number of searchlights about, I don't remember seeing one of them. I was looking up all the time to find the enemy silhouetted against the bright moonlit sky.

We'd just popped above a thin layer of cloud – and there was the Dornier, a sort of grey colour. I fired a long burst, and saw an explosion behind the pilot's cockpit. It seemed to go straight down, and I tried to follow, so steeply that the observer came out of his seat. When the Dornier crashed, three brilliantly white blobs appeared to jump out of the ground. That was Dornier number one. The next patrol nothing happened at all, except my observer complaining about the hardness of his seat.

We got Dornier number two during the second alert. It must have been about four in the morning. He was travelling very fast and jinking violently. He didn't keep a straight course for more than a few seconds at a time. But there was no cloud about now, it was a good night for interception, and I managed to get in a fairly long burst. He caught fire and slowed up very quickly. I got so close to him that I was caught in his slipstream and rolled on to my back, but I managed to avoid colliding with him. By the time we were right way up again he'd hit the ground and was blazing away.

Then came Dornier number three. Again I got in a long burst amidships. There was a yellowish explosion, and down he went. As he did so he fired about a second's burst, two streams of red tracer, but they went nowhere near us.

Number four was a Junkers 88, and the most spectacular of the night. We found him somewhere in the Croydon area. My cannon shells set both his engines on fire, and flames spread along the wing and back to the fuselage. They lit up the sky so clearly that we could see his black crosses. And we saw four of the crew bale out, one after the other. As it went down you could see all the streets lit up, and when it hit there was a terrific flash.

Well, that was that. Four in a night. Home we went, pleased of course, but chiefly wondering what sort of luck the rest of the squadron had had.

7. NIGHT INTRUDER

I'm afraid the dangers and hazards of flying on night offensive patrols have been rather exaggerated. Certainly the average intruder pilot is not the cat-eyed, carrot-eating killer that the Press sometimes makes him out to be. Most of us night fighters are too fond of our mornings in bed to go flying around in the daytime. Personally, sleeping in the sun appeals to me infinitely more than chasing Me. 109s at 30,000 feet. Give me a moonlight night and my old Hurricane, and you can have your Spitfires and dawn readiness. We've no formation flying to worry about, and no bombers to escort. In fact, nothing to do but amuse ourselves once we've crossed the French coast.

I must admit that those miles of Channel with only one engine brings mixed thoughts, and one can't help listening to every little beat of the old Merlin as the English coast disappears in the darkness. I always get a feeling of relief and excitement as I cross the French coast and turn on the reflector sight, knowing that anything I see then I can take a crack at. We have to keep our eyes skinned the whole time, and occasionally glance at the compass and clock. As the minutes go by and we approach the Hun aerodrome, we look eagerly for the flare paths. More often than not we are disappointed. The flare path is switched off as soon as we arrive, and up come the searchlights and flak. But if you're lucky, it's a piece of cake.

The other night I saw the Jerries when I was still some distance away. They were flying round at about 2,000 feet. I chose the nearest and followed him round. He was batting along at about 200 miles an hour, but I soon caught him, and got him beautifully lined up in my sights before letting him have it.

The effect of our four cannon is incredible, after the eight machine-guns I had previously been used to. Scarcely had I pressed the button when a cluster of flashes appeared on the bomber and a spurt of dark red flame came from its starboard engine. The whole thing seemed to fold up then and fall out of the sky, burning beautifully. I turned steeply to watch it crash, and as I did so I saw another Hun about a mile away, coming straight for me. In half a minute he was in my sights, and a second later his port petrol tank was blazing. I gave him another short burst for luck and then flew beside him. It was just like watching a film. A moment before he hit the ground, I could see trees and houses lit up by the dark red glow from the burning machine. Suddenly there was a terrific sheet of flame, and little bits of burning Heinkel flew in all directions.

I was beginning to enjoy myself by this time and flew straight back to the aerodrome to find another. Unfortunately, all the lights had been switched off, and though I circled for some time I found nothing. So I cracked off for home. I looked back once and could still see the two bombers burning in the distance, and a few searchlights trying vainly to find me. On the way back I spotted a train. They're easy to see in the moonlight, as the trail of steam shows up nicely against the dark background. I made sure it was a goods train before attacking the engine, which I left enveloped in a cloud of steam. My squadron has rather specialised in this train-wrecking racket. During the April-May full moon we blew up seventeen engines for certain, and probably several others.

Well, when your petrol and ammunition are nearly gone, you are faced with the old Channel again. If you've got something, as I had that night, you leave the enemy territory with a sort of guilty conscience; not for what you've done – that's great fun – but somehow you feel they've got it in for you, and that everyone's going to shoot at you. It's a sort of nervous reaction, I suppose. The whole thing seems too easy to be true. Ten to one there's no Hun within shooting distance, and the ground defences are quiet. That makes it all the worse, and I generally weave about till I'm half-way back across the Channel. If you've done nothing, of course, you don't get this feeling, as you're still looking for something at which to empty your ammunition – trains inland and barges and ships on the coast. We've had some of these recently, too.

Out over the Channel you can hear your ground station calling the other aircraft of the squadron, and you count the minutes and look eagerly for the coast. Often it seems to take so long coming back that you feel sure the compass is wrong. At last, in the distance, you see the flashing beacon, and soon you are taxi-ing in to your dispersal point. I dread the look of disappointment on my mechanic's face if my guns are unfired. But if the rubber covers have been shot off, I've scarcely time to stop my engine before I am surrounded by the boys asking what luck I've had. Then comes the best part of the whole trip – a cup of tea and a really good line-shooting session.

My whole squadron, both ground crews and pilots, are as keen as mustard, and I must say they've put up a terrific show. Since April 1st the squadron has destroyed 11 aircraft for certain and probably three more, apart from the 17 trains and the odd boat I mentioned before.

The lion's share of this total goes to my Czech Flight Commander, Kuttelwascher. He and I are great rivals at the game. All the boys love him. He's a first-class pilot, and has the most uncanny gift of knowing just which aerodrome the Huns are going back to. He'll look at the map and say, 'I'll go there to-night!' – possibly it is some unobtrusive Hun aerodrome. Sure enough, even if the others see no activity, old Kuttel certainly will. One night last week we agreed to visit a certain aerodrome, but five minutes before we took off he changed his mind and went to another. I got to my aerodrome to find it covered with fog, while he calmly knocked down three.

8. 'WE ALWAYS ATTACK THE ENGINE FIRST'

For three months now my squadron has been paying special attention to Mussolini's pride and joy, the electric railway from Naples which goes right round the toe of Italy as far as Taranto. Our beat on this line is from Naples about 200 miles down to Reggio Calabria, and some of the boys specialise in the steam line on the north coast of Sicily. In two nights of the March moon period the squadron shot up 32 trains. There are lots of them about.

I've done quite a bit of train-busting in France and Holland, and I got rather a shock when we went over to Italy because the mountains make life different. We always go hunting trains on bright moonlight nights, and it's really a delight to see the snow on the mountains in the toe of Italy. One of the most conspicuous landmarks is Stromboli. It's nothing but a large rock sticking out of the Mediterranean, but even in the moonlight it has a whitish-grey plume of smoke in the shape of a mushroom, and you can also see the grey lava crawling down the side of the mountain. It is a different sort of business from flying in flat countries: here you may have to circumvent 11,000 feet of Etna. It also makes the job itself a bit more difficult, because there are lots of tunnels down the Italian coast, and it's very annoying when you're hunting a train and it disappears into a tunnel and refuses to come out on the other side.

It would be nice if you could find your trains with the assistance of a time-table, but I think this line is so disorganised that the time-table wouldn't be any use anyway. We've seen quite a lot of steam trains lately, perhaps because we've put so many electric locomotives out of action. You can see the steam trains even more easily in moonlight, because of the long white trail coming out of the funnel.

If it's an electric train, you look for the flashes from the electric rail and then perhaps you circle to make your attack and you come down to zero feet and give the locomotive a good burst of cannon and machine-gun fire. You don't fire until you're on the top of the target, and you know you're going to hit it. When the cannon shell strike the rails, they throw up bright colours and flashes which light up the mountain sides. When you succeed in stopping the train, the driver will probably jump out and take cover in some convenient hill. Then you go on with your attack until you are sure that the train will stay there for a long time and give everybody the maximum amount of trouble; and then you go looking for another.

We always attack the engine first, and then, if it's a goods train, we pay great attention to what it's carrying. Some of the squadron have shot up ammunition with great effect, but what's given me the most delight is shooting up petrol. When you shoot up a petrol train the whole train goes up in flames. It's not a thing you can really describe and not easily come by, but it's very satisfactory when you do get one.

My biggest bag in one night was three trains, but they weren't petrol trains. Sometime we hope to find the place where they dump all the locos we've damaged and give them some more.

One night of the full moon last month I was fortunate enough to derail a train near Milazzo near Sicily, and it stayed there for at least 24 hours. It was a steam train going towards Palermo on a flat stretch, running fast. I made my first attack head-on. When you attack head-on the surprise effect is more beneficial. I gave it a three-second burst which stopped the engine, and a lot of steam and sparks came from it. But I turned round and made two more attacks head-on, and my observer said I'd derailed the train. That didn't seem very likely, so I went back to have another look. We actually tipped up on one wing and flew alongside just at roof level, and sure enough the train was derailed.

The Mosquito is a lovely aircraft for this sort of thing – very light and manoeuvrable on the controls, with a formidable hitting power. In my opinion Jerry hasn't an aircraft anything the equal of this.

III

INTERLUDE: FERRY COMMAND AT WORK

Picture a rather dingy room with dull brown walls; and on the brown walls maps, charts, and diagrams, and a list of instructions to pilots. In short, a typical weather-forecasting office on an aerodrome. Not a very romantic setting, you might think. But you'd be wrong. This is the king of Met. offices, for the airport it serves is one from which American bombers are ferried over the Atlantic to Britain.

On this particular afternoon the room was crowded with Air Force pilots, navigators, and radio operators; and facing them was the chief meteorologist himself.

'What are the chances for to-night, sir?' someone was asking him. Impatiently we waited for the meteorologist's reply.

Impatiently, because for seven days now we'd been waiting at the God-forsaken airport to ferry a consignment of bombers across the Atlantic to Britain. Each morning, each afternoon, our little party of pilots, navigators, and radio operators had straggled across the snow to the Met. office to get the weather forecast. And each morning, each afternoon, there seemed to be a snag. If the weather overhead was good, then it was bad over England. If Britain was basking in sunshine, our own weather would be completely closed-in.

After a week of this kind of thing, we were almost at the point of digging ourselves in for the duration. But to-day the meteorologist had a surprise for us.

'The chances are pretty good for to-night,' he announced. 'Tail winds most of the way, a high pressure area over the British Isles, and reasonably clear weather at this end. Let's look at the weather map...'

So – to-night was the night!

As soon as the meteorologist had given us his forecast there was a hum of activity: navigators and pilots settled down to work out a 'flight plan' – a flight plan, by the way, is a complete summary of the courses to be steered and the times each course will take, assuming the forecasted winds to be correct. Fragments of conversation disentangled themselves.

'What speed shall we be climbing at, sir?'

'Three hundred feet a minute – if we can.'

'How about this big cloud bank in the middle? Where do you want us to start climbing?'

'Better allow plenty of time. H'm. Say longitude 30.'

Meanwhile the radio operators were being given the code of the day, in which all messages would be sent and received. It was also their job to order our rations of soup, coffee, and sandwiches, a highly important part of the proceedings!

Two hours later everything was ready, and in the evening sunlight we ploughed our way through the snow to the runway where our planes were standing.

Nothing romantic about the inside of '272,' the medium bomber which is to carry Gilmore and 'Rod' and me across the Atlantic. In fact, her main cabin rather resembles a lumber room: kitbags, flying suits, and boots are piled in the rear; amidships there's a rubber dinghy and a great auxiliary fuel tank to starboard, and on the port side a rack of flame floats and sea markers for navigation purposes.

We picked our way past these to the forward cabins, and as navigator I went down into the little glass-fronted cubby-hole in the nose and began to put charts and instruments in their right places. It was hard to realise as we went about our routine preparations that we were going on a trip we should remember all our lives.

Despite the fact that it was our pilot's first Atlantic crossing, he was as cool and matter-of-fact as if he were going a mere 50-mile flip in a Tiger Moth. 'I think it's the attitude of mind that counts in this sort of thing,' he had told us, and certainly he set us an example of perfect serenity which couldn't fail to give confidence.

At last all was ready. Rod got busy with his radio.

'272 to Control Tower. May we take off, please?'

Yes, we could take off. And five seconds later we did, in a roaring rush down the wide runway, rising very slowly to avoid any difficulty with our big load of fuel.

After a few brief glimpses of lakes and bush we were flying above cloud, and from then until we reached the other side the world outside ceased to matter. Except for that short and wonderful interval when the setting sun turned the cloud-tops to a sea of flame. There is little time, as a rule, to enjoy the beauties of Nature when you are flying, but here was something that cried out to be admired and wondered at. You could not help catching your breath for a moment at the sight of these vast shining plains of gold, remote and infinitely serene.

Then night closed down, and we three became dwellers in a tiny world of our own. Down in my cabin in the nose (reached by three steps from the pilot's compartment) one had no sense of travelling across the Atlantic at three miles a minute; no sense of the ocean below or of the winds. You didn't realise, except when the stars became obscured, the presence of those clouds whose tops reached more than 20,000 feet into the air. True, there was glass in front of you and under your feet, but it revealed nothing but blackness beyond. Much more real was the green-walled cabin, with its roof-light cheerfully illuminating table, charts, and instruments. True again there was the constant roar of 1,000 horse-power motors, but after a very short time the ears became deaf to these; in fact, the only occasion when you were reminded of them was when their vibration juddered chart or instruments off the table.

At last we began to draw near that big cloud wall of which the meteorologist had warned us. Very soon we should have to climb up to at least 20,000 feet, unless we wanted to get tossed about like a shuttlecock by the dangerous currents inside the cloud. 'We'll have our supper first, though,' said the pilot. And if you want to know why he said that, imagine trying to eat with an oxygen mask over your face.

You see, at high level it's absolutely essential to wear an oxygen mask. If you don't you will soon be overtaken by a comfortable sleepy sensation, as if you had had too many drinks; and you will probably be incapable of realising what is the matter. Finally you will fall asleep – probably for the last time in your life.

How did we know that we had got to the point when we must start climbing? Well, of course we knew where we ought to be from the calculations we had made before the flight, based on the speed and direction of the forecast winds. The navigator's job on the flight was to check the track of the aircraft from time to time, and for some considerable distance out he could get his position from the bearings on wireless stations secured by the radio operator. After a time, distance makes it impossible to get accurate bearings, and then you are left alone with the stars and your Air Almanac.

Do you know the Air Almanac, that wonderful publication which shows you how to convert the altitude of a star into a bearing? On its cover it has the motto, 'Man is not lost,' but when first you look inside at the wilderness of figures, you don't feel so sure about that.

This business of taking sights on stars is a rather tiresome one when you are a raw navigator in an unfamiliar plane. First you have to climb up out of your cabin, pass through the pilot's compartment, and get into the main cabin, where the astro-hatch is. That sounds easy, doesn't it? But remember that you are still wearing your oxygen mask, with about five yards of rubber tubing hanging from your face. Do you recall the gentleman in Grimm's Fairy Tales who couldn't stop his nose from growing? Well, that's just what it feels like. Stumbling over your tubing, you pick your way aft, only to find when you get there that you don't know where the light switch is. But at last you find it, and the next job is to open the hatch in the roof and fasten it back. At once a draught of air at a temperature of 30 degrees below freezing point blows smartly in and fills the cabin; and in a little while your breath is turning to ice crystals inside your oxygen mask.

To the noise of the engine there is now added a strange booming roar as the wind rushes over the hole in the roof, like a giant playing on a big bass flute. By this time you are feeling strongly that you don't want to bother with taking any sights after all. However, you pull yourself together, look at your watch, raise your sextant to your eye, and train it, let us say, on Arcturus. At this precise moment Arcturus decides to retire shyly behind a thin haze, the top of that great heap of cloud I mentioned earlier. So there you are! Until Arcturus chooses to reappear, you have got to wait and nurse your impatience.

But at last, despite all these typical inconveniences, I had taken sights on two or three stars. The only task remaining was to scramble back to my cabin, work out their bearings by the Air Almanac tables, and plot the position lines which they gave.

This job was repeated, once, twice; and each time the evidence seemed to show that we were going steadily north of our track. Now came the supreme act of faith for a raw and untried navigator – to alter course sharply in the middle of the Atlantic on what was bound to seem to him rather hypothetical information. However, we did so, soon after the sun had risen.

The sea of white cloud-tops below us soon became visible again, and it was not long before the heat of the sun's rays had transformed the cabin into a kind of greenhouse.

Suddenly the pilot (I was beside him just then) pointed down. 'Land, isn't it?' he said. Sure enough, there it was, a coastline visible through a hole in the clouds. There was not time to be excited, for we still had the job of finding out exactly where on that coastline we were. It took us some time to pick up our bearings, but with the help of Rod and his radio we did it at last, found our airport, and landed. Strange to think, as one looked round at the green airfield basking in spring sunshine and warmth, that it was but a few short hours' journey from the snow-covered bush country that we left last night.

I need hardly add that our landing caused no excitement, no fuss. Why should it? No. 272 was just another aircraft in the great stream which is flowing across from the New World to Britain.

IV
HUNTING THE HUNTERS

'I seek my prey in the waters.'

1. U-BOAT WRITTEN OFF

This was our 30th operational trip and our wireless operator was on his 400th hour of operational flying. Apparently the Navy had got wind of a U-boat, and we were ordered off on an anti-submarine sweep. We took off in a gale and were ready for a pretty rough trip. But everything went uneventfully for several hours until the last half-hour of our patrol. Then I spotted moonlight shining on a breaker in a peculiar way. I still can't say just why it was peculiar. It just was.

'Hallo, Number One,' I called upon the inter-com. 'What's that funny patch of water half a mile to starboard?'

'I don't know, I'll have a look,' my captain replied. He's a slow-speaking, quick-thinking Devonian with Irish blood on one side. Only people who know him as well as we do realise that he can act about one hundred times as fast as he talks.

Just then I thought, 'Damn, it's only a patch of moonlight. I've boobed again.' By this time the patch was drifting right down the path of the moon, and then I saw a lovely streamlined shape slide into view just below and behind us.

'It's a submarine!' I yelled.

'Lord, it's a U-boat!' Number One exclaimed.

Number Two, the second pilot, was at the controls. My captain directed operations from the front turret and Number Two followed them so fast it was as though they were one man. We swept down and dived on that U-boat, hoping to catch it where our stick of depth charges could do most good. The run-up was a beauty. The first two depth charges dropped rather behind, but the third fell just aft of where the conning-tower had disappeared.

The explosion of this last was a wonderful sight. First, a splash; then a blue-green flash and a gigantic plume of smoke and water with a base as if somebody were flashing a gigantic flint gas-lighter.

I saw a 200-feet high plume of smoke and water belch up into the sky. We had dived down to drop the depth charges and had climbed to about 400 feet when the third went off. It seemed to be trying to blow us out of the sky as well.

Number Two steep-turned as though he were flying a Spitfire instead of the heavy bomber, and we made a third run over the target dropping some more depth charges into the perimeter of a 200-foot circle of troubled water.

I feel convinced that particular U-boat won't hunt again.

Did we whoop as we turned for home!

2. EIGHT SIGHTED, SEVEN ATTACKED

That was the best day's hunting I've ever had. Several times I've sighted three U-boats in a day, and we've had a crack at two. But eight sightings and seven attacks made the others seem comparatively tame.

The submarines kept bobbing up all over the place, and I began to wonder if the entire German U-boat fleet was concentrated round this one convoy. It certainly seemed like that at the time, for we'd no sooner finished one attack and got all the details logged, than another submarine would show up.

But I'd better begin when we arrived over the convoy just as dawn was breaking. We knew there were U-boats around and we were keeping our eyes skinned. The visibility wasn't too good. There was a sort of half light, and a hailstorm didn't improve things. I started my patrol by making a wide sweep round the convoy, and almost at once we struck lucky. Astern of the ships and on the Liberator's port beam I spotted a sub travelling fast on the surface. It was going all out to catch up with the convoy. I got into position to attack and, just as we dived on it, the submarine began to go down in a hurry. I didn't see what happened after the depth charges were dropped. My navigator told me they straddled the sub and hid it in showers of spray.

When we got round again, there was nothing to be seen of the U-boat, but there was a great patch of oil – about 800 yards long, I'd say it was. And in the middle of the oil there was a lot of debris – little yellow pieces of wood.

A corvette from the convoy came across and poked around and I waited for a message from it. The best way of telling whether you've sunk a U-boat is by examination of the debris, and that's not so easy to do in an aircraft. But it's all right for a ship. I was a bit anxious as I circled the corvette. Then its signal lamp flashed up at us with the message, 'You certainly got him.' A few seconds later they sent another message, 'You killed him'; and before the

corvette left to go back to the convoy it signalled, 'Dead bodies seen.'

We carried on with the patrol. It was three hours later I saw another U-boat. Actually there were two of them about 300 yards apart heading for the convoy. One of the subs was leaking oil and I went for that one. The depth charges plumped down beside it just after it had gone under, and after the explosions died away a spout of water shot high into the air.

We were having lunch when the next one appeared. I had a plate of steak and potatoes on my knee at the time, and the plate, steak, and potatoes went rolling on the floor as I grabbed the controls to put the Liberator into a dive. The submarine started to submerge, and as the deck was disappearing we opened up at it with our cannon and machine guns and peppered the conning tower pretty thoroughly.

Then came numbers five, six, seven, and eight. We did the same with them – shot them up with our guns and forced them under. It was getting dark when we turned for home. By the time we got back we'd been in the air for nearly seventeen hours. We were pretty hungry, too, but it was worth losing our lunch to sink a U-boat and attack six more.

3. SUNDERLAND'S MIXED BAG

On my first operational flight I sank an R-boat. They are small motor launches used for various jobs – escort duty and mine-laying. This one was about 78 feet long. We were right down in the corner of the Bay of Biscay, patrolling not far from the French coast. We were nearing the end of our patrol. There were some Spanish trawlers about which we inspected very carefully. We saw this boat about 5 to 8 miles away. He looked innocent enough until he started turning and twisting. So we dived past him at a respectable distance to inspect him, and through the glasses we identified him as a German naval craft. He clapped on all speed and so did we. He didn't get much of a chance to fire at us. We climbed up to attack.

It was my first action. My hair was standing on end, but it's always like that. Every time I sight the enemy I have a feeling that I've nearly trodden on a snake. You're going to get him and kill him, but meanwhile you've got to step back from the danger. We climbed up ready to attack and positioned ourselves. I took over the controls then, and he was so agile that the only way to attack him was to dive-bomb him. We did this. We dived twice and machine-gunned him heavily. They seemed to be too disorganised to return the fire effectively. Then we did two dive-bombing attacks and released a stick of bombs, pulling out fairly low and going at a terrific speed, and we could see him lifted clean out of the water by the explosions, and he fell back into the water pretty badly battered. The tail gunner called out, 'Tell the captain we've blown hell out of him.' We attacked again. When the spray cleared away from the second attack – almost a direct hit – we saw them throwing life-boats and dinghies overboard and abandoning ship. We ceased fire then and watched the boat listing heavily to port and sinking by the stern, while about half a dozen survivors were swimming away as rapidly as possible.

I had it in mind to go down and rescue the survivors, but at this stage enemy fighters appeared on the scene, and I had to take avoiding action. By the time I got clear our petrol supply was so low that all we could do was to set course for home. We were all very excited about our first action, but by the time the day was over we were so tired that all we could do was to turn in and go to bed. It's always like that when you have an action.

As a matter of fact, between the middle of March and the end of October we've had a rather lively time – much more so than most of the crews. Besides our first R-boat, we managed to sink two submarines and damage three others and damage two merchant ships; we've also been involved in a number of air actions. I have known of crews that have gone out for a year and not even seen a U-boat, so we've been rather lucky. Our first U-boat we didn't even see. We were patrolling in the Bay of Biscay when I saw a trail of oil bubbles two or three miles away. It was about 100 yards long, so he hadn't very long submerged. We weren't sure at first if it was a U-boat, but we examined it very closely and found it was moving at a U-boat's usual speed under water. We didn't know how far down the U-boat was. We attacked with depth charges. Now there was no doubt at all in our minds about its being a U-boat, because a great flood of oil came up and spread in a widening pool and later fairly big air bubbles came up in the middle of the oil.

We were wildly excited now, because we had apparently damaged him to some degree, and although the trail of oil moved on and changed direction sharply, we were sure the damage was real. We followed him for some time, making careful measurements as to speed so that we could make our next attack as accurate as possible. We followed him for some six miles before we attacked again. Again he altered course and a huge quantity of oil came up, spreading in a widening patch, and some minutes later still more air bubbles, quite large ones, rose to the surface. We were out of bombs by this time, but another aircraft was sent out to relieve us, and we signalled to them giving them every possible detail to help with their attack. We just had time to see them attack before we had to turn for home as our petrol was getting low. We couldn't stay long enough to see the results of their attack, but we know that, between us, we maintained contact until after dark, and he must have been rather crippled by then because my relief aircraft reported that his speed was reduced and his course was very erratic. On the way back I couldn't help feeling sorry for the crew of the U-boat, being hammered again and again and not knowing when or where the assault was coming from.

The first U-boat that we knew for certain that we had sunk was in the Mediterranean when I was operating from Gibraltar, shortly after the other action. We were out on patrol to cover an area where a U-boat had been attacked the previous day. There was a dead flat calm. We sighted a big Italian U-boat dead ahead cruising fast on the surface. I immediately dived at maximum speed. There was the mad moment of feverish activity that always follows my sounding the submarine attack alarm, which blares throughout the aircraft and startles everybody into action. Everyone jumps to their routine job at action stations. An extraordinary number of things get done in a surprisingly few seconds. We dived at maximum speed to get him before he crash-dived. When we were about half a mile away, he showed no signs of crash-diving, so we thought we'd taken him by surprise, coming dead astern. But suddenly there was a bright flash and a loud explosion as a big shell burst dead ahead of us. We got a terrific surprise and pulled away into a steep climbing turn which shot us up about 2,000 feet, with flak and machine-gun bullets bursting all round us and sometimes hitting us. My tail gunner was so furious that, unconsciously taking up his microphone, he reeled off a string of good Australian abuse in such a loud voice that I had to stop him because he was monopolising the wire without realising it.

We circled the submarine, and studied every detail of its construction, especially the placing of the guns, so as to plan an attack which would be as safe as possible. We attacked him with bombs and machine-gunned him heavily, but he turned sharply to port and we missed him. We were under machine-gun fire throughout the attack. Our port bomb racks were not working, but during the action and while we were under fire, my armourer, L.A.C. Bob Scott, with the help of some of the crew, carried the bombs from the port racks to those on the starboard side, which were now empty, so that we could make another attack. He well deserved the D.F.M. that he got for this action. In fact, the whole crew were simply marvellous.

We made a second attack, but the U-boat's fire forced us to turn aside before we could drop any bombs: however, my gunners poured a hail of accurate fire at point-blank range into the U-boat's conning tower, which was very crowded. Finally we attacked him with our remaining bombs, diving very low over him, in spite of his accurate fire. A stick of bombs fell diagonally across him and plumb centre. That stopped him all right, and he lay with no movement for some minutes while we machine-gunned him heavily. We had to return to base, but we know that the U-boat never got home. Our Sunderland was fairly badly shot up, but none of us had a scratch.

I said that we've been lucky in our boat because we've seen a lot of action. As a matter of fact I think that about 35 per cent. of our patrols have involved us in some action or other. We're rather disappointed if we have an uneventful patrol. We feel reluctant to leave the patrol area unless we've seen something of the enemy. I was trying to think what the feeling was like when it suddenly occurred to me that it's like going fishing. If the fish aren't biting you want to stop on and on until you get some sort of a catch, and that's just how all of us feel. All my crew are as keen as mustard, and they really are disappointed when we have a quiet patrol.

The way I look at it is this. The U-boats are certain to be there somewhere, and it's a battle of wits between them and us. If we are more cunning and keen-eyed than the U-boat's crew, we will see them first and be able to attack. If they see us they can get away, so if we let the boredom of uneventful patrols make us relax and spoil our enthusiasm, we simply won't get the results. So we've given a lot of thought to working out a technique by which we keep an efficient look-out and use the sun and cloud cover to our own advantage. But the technique is no good unless the crew are keen, and my crew are. You can't stop studying anti-submarine warfare. The whole of my crew eat, drink, sleep, and dream U-boats, and I believe that's been the chief thing in getting our bag.

Now with surface ships it's different. They can't crash-dive, but their fire is more deadly than that of a U-boat, so we have to use different methods. The two ships we damaged were a naval supply vessel of 6,000 tons and a merchant vessel converted into a flak ship. We attacked these, making our dive from a height of several thousand feet, and we managed to score hits and near misses on each before leaving them. When we attacked the naval supply vessel we saw his bows lift clean out of the water. We couldn't stop to see the final result as our engines were damaged by his fire, but his speed was considerably reduced, and it was obvious that he had fairly severe damage below the water-line. By the way, before we attacked him he tried to trick us. When we had sighted him first about 12 miles away there was a U-boat alongside which dived immediately and disappeared. As we came closer, the ship ran up the British red ensign and put out in various conspicuous places R.A.F. roundels or rings. Pretending to be bluffed we flew round in a friendly fashion while we made a careful inspection of the ship and at the same time kept a look-out for any signs of the U-boat. Just when we had made sure of our quarry we went straight into the attack and caught him napping through his own bluff.

The most exciting time we have had was when we sank our second U-boat. We saw him a long way off and were able to stalk him through the clouds. In the last stage of our attack there was a small cloud between us and him, so we used it as a protection and dived through it to come out a mile and a half from him, and take him so completely by surprise that he couldn't crash-dive in time to avoid my attack. In fact, I was able to turn away and wait until he was about to disappear under the surface. Then I released my bombs right across his bows. I knew we'd got him, because I could see every inch of the U-boat under the surface, and we all saw him run into the bombs as they exploded, just as we got clear. We circled the position, and after the commotion from the bombs had subsided, huge streams of air bubbles arose, seething on the surface like an immense kettle boiling furiously, and this went on for some minutes. Large quantities of thick oil covered the area. The U-boat must have gone straight to the bottom. We knew that we had hit him with several bombs.

4. 'THE MINE JUST SITS THERE, WAITING PATIENTLY'

Every now and then you may have heard a little phrase at the end of the Air Ministry's communiqués: 'Mines were laid in enemy waters.'

It may be that you haven't taken a great deal of notice of those few rather colourless words. All the same, they describe one of the most useful parts of the work being done by our bombers to-day.

I was taking part in this work the other night in one of our bombers. We droned away for those enemy waters in which our dangerous seed was to be sown. A mine is really a sort of delayed-action bomb dropped into the water. You see it flop out of the aircraft and go sailing down on its parachute. It sinks into the water very quietly; no flame, no flash, no leaping debris such as a big bomb may make. The mine just sits there waiting, very, very patiently. It may wait for only a few hours. It may wait months. But if during all that time a ship comes anywhere near it, the mine will get it. Just think what it means to the enemy, that night after night British aircraft buzz round that long coastline from Narvik to Bordeaux, along which must go his vital convoys carrying the slave-produced goods of occupied Europe.

The convoys must hug the shores, or else our bombers, motor torpedo boats, or submarines will get them. But along the shore in the shallow waters the mine-layers have been at work the night before. It was a dirty night on which we went, with cloud down to within a few hundred feet above the sea. We flew above it. Up there it was a lovely starlit evening with a young moon hanging in the light western sky. The trouble with flying above cloud like that is, of course, that you may not be able to tell where you are. And your mine must be dropped just where you want it. However, for us that night the question largely solved itself. As soon as we reckoned that we were off the enemy coast we began to see searchlights and flak. Those of our crew who had been in these parts a good many times before had little difficulty in placing themselves. Soon we found a flak barrage going up to port as well as to starboard. That told us definitely where we were. Down through the cloud we went, lower and lower; the altimeter seemed to be trying to knock its bottom out. At last we came out of the greyness, and then just a few feet below was the sea, rough and brown and cold, and too near for comfort. Back we went into cloud.

'Bomb doors open.'

'Clonk.'

'Mine gone.'

'Bomb doors shut.'

On the way home I thought, 'Well, it's there. Probably, of course, the enemy knows these channels are now dangerous. But that means that all his convoys will have to put into port. For days, probably, a fleet of mine-sweepers will have to come out seeking for what we have dropped. Maybe they won't find it. Maybe our mine will be detected and swept up. But then, just as the channels are clear again, the next dark night they will hear the drone of our bombers.

They will wonder if all these channels aren't dangerous again. And maybe they will be, or maybe somewhere else will be. Then they will have to decide whether to send the convoys through and risk half a dozen laden ships going to the bottom, or start their sweeping all over again.

For this is one of the great advantages of this new method of dropping mines from aircraft. If you think of it, a minelayer or a submarine cannot revisit a minefield once it has been laid. For if it did it would probably be blown up on its own mines. But an aircraft can come back and back, keeping up the supply as it were, relaying just as the sweeping is done. Aircraft mining is a good example of the intimate co-operation between the Navy and the Air Force. The whole thing is planned at the Admiralty as part of our general programme of mining, by all sorts of agencies. We of the Air Force are the delivery agents as it were. Every now and then they tell us about the results. Information seeping through from Europe tells us of new wrecks along the coast, convoys held up, supplies dislocated, ships diverted to mine-sweeping.

So when you next hear that, 'Mines were laid in enemy waters,' feel a little pleased that something very awkward and unpleasant, and something which he simply cannot stop, is being done to the enemy.

V
ORDEAL BY WATER

'I would hasten my escape from the windy storm and tempest.'
The Psalmist

1. THE LINE SQUALL

We were near Freetown, West Africa, on convoy duty when a tropical storm broke. What we call a 'line squall.' It's really difficult to describe except to say that it's one of the most terrifying things that you can see. There's an enormous wall of black cloud rising sixteen or eighteen thousand feet into the air. It forms a definite line over the sea at about a thousand feet above water level, and there's a succession of water spouts – one every hundred yards or so – running up to the bottom of the cloud layer. The line of this storm was 120 miles long, and it was about 30 miles thick.

When you meet a thing like that there are two things you can do. One is to go straight through it at low level. If you do that you fly through something that seems like solid water. It's as black as night and the wind will toss your aircraft all over the sky, and then smash you down again to within a hundred or two feet above the sea. In these terrific ups and downs your instruments stop working, and you're practically flying blind with no instruments to help you; and when you come down you do actually bounce on the cushion of the ascending air currents.

The other way is to try and get round the storm, and that's what I tried to do on this occasion. I flew along the line with one wing tip actually in the wall. The line really is as sharp as that. And when you do that you can feel the turbulence of the inner edge of the wall. At one time we were flying along the edge of this immense wall with the engines throttled back, registering a 1,500-feet-a-minute climb and 175 knots on the clock. And remember that our cruising speed is about 130. That shows you what the air currents were like.

Well, something went wrong with the engines, and I saw that I should have to come down on the water. There was a 20-foot sea running, a short steep sea, and it was quite impossible to land across it. I tried to stall the aircraft to come straight down flat, but we bounced about 50 feet into the air and dropped about 70 feet between the next two seas, with such a crash that the aircraft broke her back just behind the pilot's seat, and though I didn't know it at the time I fractured my spine. I'd given the eleven members of the crew the warning, and one of them had gone along to the bomb room to try to put the depth charges to safe, because they were all fused to go off in fairly shallow water. I'm afraid we never saw him again. The rest of us climbed on to the top of the aircraft, which was sinking rapidly.

When I got on top of the aircraft my legs collapsed. The hull was rapidly filling, and we had no dinghy to take us off. It was then that Warrant Officer Shakes of Wellington, New Zealand, and Sergeant Prior of Hove dived into the aircraft into about eight feet of water to try to get one of the dinghies. They went through the midships gun positions and got that dinghy out, and I crawled off the wing and paddled my way to it, and the crew helped me in. This was only a very small dinghy meant for three people, but we pushed off as quickly as we could because we were afraid the depth charges might go off at any moment. We had a couple of aluminium paddles, and we used those, and the rest of them swam alongside the dinghy pushing it along, while the aircraft was carried away with the drift of the sea. There wasn't much to take stock of on that dinghy, in fact, the only provisions we had were three tins of tomato juice between ten men. Our next disaster was two hours after, when a leather thong on the dinghy broke and part of the rubber ballooned and burst. So now only half the dinghy was left. We lashed up the deflated side so that two people could, lie on it, mostly under water, and one other could lie on the inflated side. By this time we had evolved a system. We decided that every man after three hours in the water could have half an hour resting on the dinghy. Of course, nearly every time that anyone climbed on to the dinghy, it was upset and the passengers were thrown into the water. We lost the paddles this way, but fortunately not before we were two miles from the aircraft. And so, when the depth charges blew up during the night, we were far enough away for safety.

The nights were the worst. They were eleven hours long. The only thing good about the nights was that it was warmer in the water than outside it.

During daylight some members of the crew were a bit troubled at the idea that there might be sharks about. I told them that it was too early in the year for sharks, and as a matter of fact, oddly enough, we saw neither shark nor barracuda, which are almost worse. The only living creatures that troubled us were dog-fish and jelly fish. Flight Sergeant Hewitt got very badly bitten, and some of the dog-fish came right up the dinghy when it was submerged and bit me while I was lying on the inflated part. I wasn't much use on this job. My second in command, Flight Lieutenant Alex Espley, from Saskatoon, really took charge of the expedition and set a magnificent example to the rest of the crew. Time after time he sacrificed his rest period in the dinghy so that someone could take it who needed it more than he thought he did himself. I reckon that of the first forty-eight hours he spent forty-five swimming alongside in his Mae West, and in the end I had to order him to the dinghy so that we could massage his legs. He was suffering extreme pain, but he simply wouldn't give in.

But they were all very fine. It was thirty-six hours before we opened the first tin of tomato juice. I shook it well and opened it myself, and you can guess how much there was between ten men; it was just a matter of wetting the palate. We had another tin in the morning.

At various times we'd seen aircraft and naval vessels even within half a mile, but we had no distress signals, as we hadn't time to retrieve them from the aircraft after the crash, and it wasn't until we'd been at sea for forty-eight hours that a Hudson found us. She'd been looking for us, and she dropped four single-seater fighter-type dinghies and some emergency rations and some water bottles lashed to Mae Wests. But the bottles dropped off as they fell, so we still had only the one tin of tomato juice.

Everybody was very weak by this time, but Hewitt and Shakes volunteered to swim and get the dinghies and the food. I suppose the farthest of them was about a quarter of a mile away, and we paddled the wreck of the dinghy after them. And then we ate malt tablet and biscuits that the Hudson had dropped, and we had some chewing gum. The Hudson told us that a destroyer would be along by 6 o'clock that evening, and on the strength of that we drank the remaining tin of tomato juice. But nothing came in sight at 6 o'clock. And night fell. It was 10.30 next morning when the Hudson and two Sunderlands found us again, but by that time one of the crew had gone out of his mind and died. An hour later the destroyer arrived and picked us up with its lifeboat. They picked up the fighter dinghies too, and even the wrecked dinghy which had supported us so well.

2. 'HER SMOKE WAS A BEAUTIFUL SIGHT'

This is the story of how the courageous crew of an Australian warship saved nine R.A.F. men, of whom I was one, from the sea. The odds were so heavy against us that it is a miracle we were not all written off.

We were the crew of a Sunderland flying boat of the Coastal Command, and a fairly mixed crowd. The captain and second pilot were Canadian, and I, the third pilot, come from Capetown. The rest hailed from the Empire and the home country.

I suppose superstitious people might deduce something from the fact that we numbered thirteen, but that didn't worry us as it is quite a normal number in a Sunderland. Incidentally, it was my first operational trip, and the navigator's too.

We had been flying through the night for over nine hours on our patrol when we set course back for the coast of Scotland, several hundred miles away. The weather was absolutely filthy with wind, rain, and mist; visibility, which matters most in the air, was practically nil. In fact, conditions were so bad that even the wireless wouldn't function because of atmospheric interference. I put the earphones on once or twice and the noise might have been an echo of what was going on outside – a rushing sound like a close-up of a mighty waterfall.

We did our best to navigate back to our base without wireless help. We climbed to 5,000 feet, where we got a bit of icing-up, and came down low when we calculated we should be near home. There was nothing in sight but sea, and we knew we were well and truly lost.

Petrol was getting very low. We had enough left for only about another 15 minutes flying, so the captain, a flight lieutenant with the D.F.C., decided to try and alight while he could still use his engines. The closer we came to the sea, the worse it looked. The waves were simply enormous. It is one of the most difficult operations in flying to land a boat successfully with anything of a sea running. If you get even a wing-tip float stove in you're finished, because she loses trim and the wing goes in.

Down we came towards the dark sea. Our normal landing speed is about 100 knots. The pilot brought her in at 50 knots to try and save the hull, and with the terrific wind our ground speed was probably not more than 20 knots. We held our breath as we touched down, but nothing came adrift. It was a really wonderful landing in almost insuperable difficulties.

Now we were tossing up and down on the huge waves, with the engines stopped and the wind whistling past like a tornado. It was still dark. The wireless operators, who had been trying ceaselessly to get into touch with the base, were tapping out messages. We learned later that these had been received, and a directional bearing obtained from them which resulted eventually in our rescue.

The motion was so violent that we were all sick except the chief air-gunner, a man of Malvern. He took long spells at the controls, using the ailerons to save the aircraft from buffeting as much as possible, while the rest of us got the dinghies prepared.

As time went by, the wind and sea were both rising. It didn't seem possible for conditions to get any worse, but they did! We'd had nothing to eat for 12 hours or so, and anyway it was impossible to keep anything down. I ate an orange, but it was no good.

When daylight came we received a wireless message that help was on the way. A ship was expected to reach us about 2.30 in the afternoon. The waiting hours were pretty anxious ones, but at 2.45 we saw her smoke. It was a beautiful sight. In driving, drizzling rain we let off distress signals. She turned towards us, and stood off a bit to make rescue preparations.

Then something happened that we had all been dreading. An enormous wave got us. I can see it coming now. The gunner was still at the controls, and he shouted, 'Look what's coming!' As it swept past us, the control column hit him in the stomach, and then went loose. Our port wing-tip and float had carried away. It was amazing that the thing hadn't happened before. The fact that we had floated securely in that sea for eight and three-quarter hours is the finest tribute possible to our captain's landing and the stout build of a Sunderland.

But now the boat was going. She heeled to port and we scrambled out on top. If it hadn't been so serious, it would have been funny to see us all throwing our heavy flying clothing into the sea – boots, parachute harness, overalls, etc. One chap held up his wool-lined boots, shook his head sadly, and dropped them gently into the sea.

The chief air-gunner climbed out on the starboard wing to try and balance the aircraft. He slipped on a patch of oil, and fell into the water. Then things happened rather quickly. We threw him ropes. The Sunderland started to turn over. I found myself in the water and tried to undo one of the dinghies. The mooring ropes got round my neck, and I thought I was going to be drowned underneath.

Our rescue-ship saw what was happening to the Sunderland and steamed to windward giving us the shelter of her lee. We were in a bunch in the sea, supported by our Mae West lifejackets, and swam and paddled towards the warship. From her deck, someone flung a lifebelt towards me. On it was painted 'H.M.A.S. *Australia*.' The crew threw out ropes and scrambling nets for us to climb up.

In a few minutes some of the *Australia*'s crew themselves were in the water with us, helping to get us aboard. I learned later that the ship's captain was among them. They assisted us to ropes, but we were paralysed with cold and could hardly hold them. Even if you'd got a rope round your arm, you were in the water one moment and pulled high out of it the next by the movement of the ship. There was always the danger of being crushed against the ship's side. Several chaps climbed partly up the rope ladders and fell back into the sea. I'm sorry to say that four of our number disappeared in those dreadful few moments, and were not seen again. Without the very gallant help of the Australians, I don't think any of us would have reached the deck.

Somehow I got on the wrong side of one of the scrambling nets, and was in imminent danger of being slapped against the ship's plates. But a sailor got hold of me through the net, and held on. Someone let down a bowline, which I got beneath my arms with the sailor's help, and the next minute I was going up to the rails like a lift. I remember noticing, half dazed, that my watch glass was cracked, and muttering, 'Damn, I've broken the glass!'

They wanted to carry me below, but with a sort of muzzy stubbornness, I insisted on walking. Of course, I had to be supported on both sides, and the officers laughingly humoured me. The nine of us who had been saved were put in the sick bay with warm blankets, hot bottles, and drinks to thaw us out. We must have been in the water round about 30 minutes, and some of us didn't stop shivering for two hours. Meantime, the search went on for the missing four, but without success.

At last we turned for the land, leaving the Sunderland floating upside down, hull awash. The seas were by then about 50 feet high, and the wind was so strong that it was right off the ship's indicator, gusting at well over 100 m.p.h. The captain, when he had dried and changed, came down and told us it was the worst storm he had seen in his life.

The crew, nearly all Australians, couldn't have been kinder to us during our two days' voyage to port. We parted from them regretfully – but it felt grand to be ashore again!

3. THREE MEN IN THE MEDITERRANEAN

The Pilot speaks: Except for Malta dog, a local germ which gives you a sharp pain behind the eyes, and the Mediterranean sandflies, the Island is a good place to work from.

The Maltese themselves are cheerful, but every time an incendiary breaks on their hard and sun-baked soil they want us to go and bomb Rome. They have the utmost contempt for the Italians, whom we could occasionally see circling around the island at a safe distance, dropping their bombs in the sea and sheering off – no doubt to shoot a tremendous line when they got back to their bases. But when they came over and our fighters brought an 'Eyetie' down, you could hear the cheering from all over the Island.

This was our twentieth operation. Once before, cannon shell had split open our petrol tank and fractured the main spar; and on another occasion, during an attack on a convoy of schooners and merchant vessels off Lampedusa, a ship carrying a gun looking like a howitzer opened up as we passed over, and lifted us bodily into the air. Our score in the Mediterranean was already three ships sunk and a fourth shared with two other aircraft, and once we had attacked a supply column on the Tripoli-Benghazi road and watched the drivers running in all directions into the desert while others took what they thought was shelter under the lorries. So that we weren't raw for this trip, and that was just as well.

We were briefed at 11 o'clock in the morning by Wing Commander Edwards, who had recently won the V.C. for going through a balloon barrage in daylight over Bremen, and he thought our target was pretty tough. That morning a reconnaissance machine had reported eight merchant vessels and four destroyers, with Macchis escorting them above. We found, instead, six merchant vessels and seven destroyers.

I was flying No. 4 in an elongated 'V' formation. My left window was open so that I could keep closer formation and get some air into the machine. Although we were flying in open shirt and shorts it was pretty warm.

I think the observer and I saw the convoy at the same moment, didn't we, Jock?

The Observer speaks: Yes. We were doing a square search and were on the last lag when we saw on the horizon a line of large ships, and Bill called out, 'Here we go.'

We batted in just above sea-level, flying in line abreast, and at full five miles away I saw the lines of tracer coming at us from the destroyers. You could see the splash, splash, splash in the water around us, and as we got really near, Tony in the rear turret had an awkward moment as the tracer lines seemed to scissor across him.

The Air-gunner speaks: 'Awkward' is putting it mildly. Anyway it was a sheet, not a line, of tracer coming from the destroyers on either side of us. It started up a few yards from our tail, slowly caught up with us, and then from my position in the turret I watched it entering the fuselage and creeping up towards me. I think another six inches and I should have had it; I could hear it ripping in like little stabs through tinfoil.

As our bomb doors sprang to and we passed over the ship I had a look at the aircraft and saw smoke. I said to Bill, 'H'm, looks like your starboard engine's on fire.' I tried to make it sound as unconcerned as I could, as though it were his aircraft and not mine, and I continued to give him a running commentary on the situation in what was meant to be a detached manner.

I took some photographs of the burning ship. I guess they were the best photos I ever took. I can safely say that, because they're 250 fathoms down and they won't be developed now. Then I smelt burning, and this time I don't think I sounded quite so detached when I told Bill. The bomb well was alight, and while I grabbed one extinguisher Jock grabbed the other.

The Observer: Yes, Tony and I were on either side of the bomb well and were spraying the flames and smoke with fluid. I think my aim was better than his because Tony got more over me than I did over him. The aircraft was pretty well filled with asphyxiating smoke, because the wireless set was also alight. I pulled away the top hatch to get rid of some of it, while Tony went on giving Bill the latest news about the fire in the starboard engine.

The Pilot: I must say it was pretty good, Tony. If it hadn't been our own aircraft that was burning, I should have been able to have taken a more objective interest in your power as a reporter. Anyway, your masterly restraint caused me to switch off the starboard engine, turn off the petrol, and open the throttle to drain it. The aircraft flew on.

I could now detect in the remaining engine a suspicious note, and she began to surge. Probably what had happened was that a bullet had got embedded in the boost control. Slowly the port engine lost power, and I asked Jock to find out our position.

The Observer: I was quite glad to have my mind taken off things, because it was a bit depressing watching the distance increase between us and the remainder of the squadron going ahead. I was taking Very cartridges out of the rack, because it was getting too hot from the fire, when I heard Bill call out that the other engine was going.

I wondered what it was going to be like. I never found out, for I suddenly went unconscious, and the next thing I knew was that I was in the water with the plane three yards away, her nose pointing at an angle downwards and her wings lying flat on the sea. I jettisoned my parachute and looked around for Bill.

The Pilot: My escape wasn't as easy as that, and for a moment I thought I wasn't going to escape at all. When I knew that L for Leather was going in, I gave her as flat a landing as possible and felt her splash into the sea. I shut my eyes and felt a great sheet of water smacking hard into me. Somehow I was turned the wrong way and found myself facing the armour plating. I felt for the pin of the Sutton harness, which releases you from the straps which tie you to the seat. Normally the pin lies across your middle, and you could find it in your sleep. Automatically I groped for it, but found it was gone. Thinking I was free, I tried to rise but couldn't get away from the straps. They were doing their job. I started searching wildly around my body for the fastening and found the pin just below the shoulders at the back, pulled it out with my right hand and the straps fell away. I floated up. How did you get out, Tony?

The Air-gunner: Well, I felt a terrific pressure on my whole body, as though every part of me was being clamped in a separate vice. Everything inside the aircraft was smashing up. Almost immediately the water level had risen, going from Bill's sliding hatch to the tail, so that I knew we were nose down. I found myself sitting in about two and a half feet of water. I opened my hatch and saw Jock swimming six yards away, with Bill ahead of me struggling to unbuckle himself from the sinking plane.

It was my job to get the dinghy out. It was floating inside the aircraft and I heaved it up. Jock and Bill used to chip me about a knife on a lanyard I always carried at my waist, and Jock shouted to me now to use this famous weapon. I cut the cord and released the dinghy. It became automatically inflated by the compressed air cylinders.

At the first crash of water I had been thrown on my back and banged my head on something hard. I didn't notice much wrong then, but now I felt that I had broken my arm and seemed to have injured my spine. Anyway, I got out and saw that Jock was in the dinghy.

The Observer: From my safe seat in the boat, Tony, you looked pretty comical. You probably don't remember it, but one of your flying boots had come off and was filled with water. You were hugging it like a mother with a baby. Do you remember, Bill, arguing with him in the water about it?

The Pilot: Do I remember! I could have crowned him with it, but nothing would make him give it up.

The Air-gunner: I know. I developed a passion for that boot and would have fought you to the last for it, in spite of my limp arm.

The Observer: Anyway, from where I was in the dinghy I could see the scene pretty clearly. Bill was helping Tony along towards the dinghy, and a few yards away I could see the tail of L for Leather slipping into the sea. Then Bill dived down and got his shoulder under Tony's seat, while I grabbed him by the shoulders and hauled him in, boot and all.

Then Bill got in and we looked at each other. The last tip of the rudder went down. Well beyond the horizon we could see the haze of smoke from the burning convoy. We made a sling for Tony from the lace of his Mae West. Bill was only scratched, although some of the skin had been torn off his legs and they were bleeding a little. We told him the salt water would help to heal them.

The Pilot: Yes, but it was stinging like blazes, and anyway you couldn't do much grinning because of the gash near your knee. You had on one shoe and one sock, torn shorts, a ripped shirt, no helmet, and a Mae West.

The Observer: I know, but I kept my watch. Both yours and Tony's were ripped off. Mine stopped at 2.25, the moment when the sea came in, and the glass was broken. I've got it here now. Anyway, we didn't do much arguing then. We said nothing for half an hour. Tony took off his remaining flying boot.

The Air-gunner: I thought what an ass I had been. I looked at both my boots sadly and thought they had done me pretty well. Then I threw them both out and wondered how long it would take them to go down 250 fathoms. We kept on looking at each other and at the dinghy, and at the sea, and at the blue sky. A breeze was coming up and there was a slight swell.

I forget who broke the silence. It was you, Bill, wasn't it?

The Pilot: I remember wondering what all our mothers would say if they could have seen us then – their devoted sons, looking a pretty odd sight, if you can think of it that way, with no water, and no food, and a few flying fish for company. But as a matter of fact, come to think of it, Jock broke the silence first. He was sick eight times. And he was so beautifully polite over it. Each time he said, 'Excuse me,' and went ahead.

The Observer: Yes, but I would like to make it clear that I wasn't being seasick. It was all that damn salt water I had swallowed.

The Pilot: Well, that's your story, Jock. Anyway, we all had to make ourselves as comfortable as we could, and unfortunately every spot on which we sat in the dinghy got a sort of dent which filled with the water dripping off us. I took off my shoes and started to bale out – in the old-fashioned sense. We took off most of our clothes to let the sun dry our bodies, and tried finding comfortable positions for our legs.

We sat away from the sea anchor, which is a kind of drag apparatus of ropes and canvas, so that the waves break under the prow of the dinghy. Jock tried to dry some cigarettes in the sun. They had got soaked from the dripping.

The Observer: It wasn't any use, because, when they dried, the paper burst. Anyway we had no matches and our one lighter wouldn't work. As the afternoon wore on, our hopes of being rescued that evening grew thin. We had been pretty certain that a Sunderland would arrive to take us off. When we first got in the dinghy the rest of the squadron came back and waggled their wings at us to show they had seen us, so we weren't in much doubt. But after a few hours we began to wonder.

We tried to take our minds off the subject by talking, mostly about beer and food. We thought of what they'd been having in Malta just then, grapes and melons and pears. And then we talked about whether we liked prickly pears. And cigarettes, of course, kept on cropping up.

Tony said we were certain to be picked up that day. We repeated that again and again. We were certain to get picked up all right. But nothing came, and then it got dark. As the night set in it became cold, and for some reason they put me in the middle.

The Air-gunner: You know the reason darn well, Jock. It was because you're the smallest and anyway you'd lost most blood. I think you were the first to go to sleep. We all dozed, on and off for a bit, and filled in time watching the fish just beneath the surface of the water. You could see the moonlight glinting on their scales.

The stars were much clearer than they are here. Three of them, part of the Plough, I knew pretty intimately. I had watched them as a kid. I remember thinking how extraordinary it was that they were the same stars that I had watched, when I was at school, and then later on from my garden at home and when I went out walking in the country. And now we were floating on a bit of rubber in the middle of the Mediterranean and looking at the same three stars. Of course it all seems damn silly now.

The Pilot: Do you remember, Tony, those flashes we saw in the night? We couldn't make out whether they were natural or from a beacon. We heard noises of aircraft, and you wanted me to let off one of our two distress signals to draw their attention.

The Air-gunner: Yes, I know, and you refused, because you said you weren't going to use them until you knew for certain they would be seen. The next day I was mighty glad. We got stiffer and stiffer throughout the night and kept on trying a different angle with our legs. We were all thankful when the sun came up.

The Observer: Yes, but don't forget about the false dawn. The sky grew faintly yellow and we thought the night had gone, and then it was all dark again. The real dawn, when it came, was sudden – first faintly red, a yellow burst, and the sun was up.

We thought we heard voices. But they were seagulls calling each other, and the flying fish started to rise again with tails like twin spines and a little bit of fin on the end. They were blue and some of them were green – shoals jumping out of the water and catching the sun on their bodies and disappearing.

The Pilot: And do you remember the turtle that morning? We eyed him hungrily at first, thinking what a good meal he'd make for breakfast. And then we were scared of him. I expect he felt the same about us – greedy at first, and then afraid. He dived down and we could see him coming under the dinghy. He had pretty sharp teeth, and he could have ripped through the rubber like a kid biting a wafer.

At ten to eight in the morning we saw a black oblong in the distance rather like an old square sail. We couldn't make it out, but it grew bigger and Tony flashed it with mirror, while I got a marine flare ready. We paddled towards it at about half a knot, and when I guessed it was the conning tower of a submarine I let the flare off and thirteen white stars climbed from it about a hundred feet into the sky.

The Observer: Yes, but don't forget we didn't know the nationality of the submarine. We could see a chap in a green shirt on the conning tower, and one in a red shirt on the hull. You said, 'Blast! They're "Eyeties"!' and we thought what a villainous couple they looked.

As they came up to us we waved and called out, 'Are you British?' A Yorkshire voice came back, 'Yes': and then, as an afterthought, 'Good show, lads.'

The Pilot: Next day the submarine put us ashore. Before we left, we were able to tell them what had happened to the convoy. After our attack a reconnaissance aircraft found there were only three merchant vessels left in the convoy. That night other bombers went out and got two more. Next day the sole survivor was found beached. We shook hands with the men of the submarine and blessed them all. They said they'd do the same again for us. Any time.

4. WINKIE THE PIGEON

When the Beaufort hit the water, I was pitched half out of the cockpit through the hatch which Mac, my navigator, had opened. He'd got the dinghy out, and for an unhappy moment he thought it wasn't going to work. But at last he managed to inflate it. The rear-gunner got his parachute harness mixed up with his guns, but he also managed to struggle clear. The rest of the crew got into the dinghy without much trouble, but I had to plop into the sea and swim for it around the front of the sinking Beaufort. Things happened so quickly that we had almost forgotten about the two pigeons in their containers. But the wireless operator remembered and got them out. He saw that chlorine gas was forming in the cockpit when sea water came into contact with the wireless batteries, and his first thought in grabbing the container and taking it into the dinghy was that he would save the pigeons from being gassed. That was a good bit of work, because one of those pigeons was largely responsible for us being rescued. This is what happened. The pigeon holder had been damaged when the Beaufort hit the sea. One of the doors was forced open, and as the wireless operator lifted the pigeons to take them into the dinghy, one of them escaped. It flew on to the fuselage, and though he tried to catch it, it stayed out of reach. Then it took off and, after circling, set course in the general direction of Scotland. We thought that was the end of Winkie, as the pigeon is called; and we had lost half our chances of rescue, because there was no message on its leg.

Mac held on to the other pigeon and when we got settled in the dinghy he wrote a message on the slip of paper in the little carrier attached to one of the pigeon's legs. It was a very gory and a very shaky message. Mac's hand had been cut and the dinghy was tossing on the waves.

After the message had been fixed to the pigeon's leg, we tossed the bird into the air and watched it disappear. That was the last we or anyone else ever saw of it. Darkness fell before it could have reached the coast, and as carrier pigeons can't fly in the dark it probably came down in the sea. But Winkie got back to Scotland and gave the aerodrome navigators a vital clue in calculating where we had come down.

Their calculations, based on the pigeon's flying speed and other information supplied by the owner of the pigeon, were very clever. A wireless SOS had been sent out before we crashed. It was faintly heard at our base, and between this and the information supplied by Winkie's owner, the navigator was able to work out approximately where we might be.

Throughout the night we steered westward by the moon and stars and a small compass I had in my pocket. It was a long night to us because we were cold and hungry. Mac wanted to sleep on the bottom of the dinghy although there was some water in it, and I had to shake him awake every now and again. We kept ourselves busy by taking 15-minute spells at the paddles, and we ate food tablets and iron rations. But I don't think we could have lasted another night.

It wasn't long after dawn when a Hudson of the Royal Netherlands Naval Air Service sighted us. It was quick work, and we have Winkie to thank for it. The Hudson dropped brandy, chocolate, water, and cigarettes in a waterproof bag, and they tasted good. Then the pilot signalled by lamp, 'What about a beer?' That was his little joke, because he didn't drop a bottle. A few hours later we were picked up by an R.A.F. rescue launch. We were given hot drinks and food and put comfortably to bed. But it must have been our lucky day, for, on the way back to port, the launch missed a floating mine by about five yards.

After we got back, the squadron had decided to make a presentation to Winkie. We had a small bronze plaque made, and it was presented to Winkie in the mess.

VI
INTERLUDE: TRAINING
IN CANADA

What advantage did we get from going to Canada for flying training? Well, first we were able to learn our job in peaceful skies where there was no balloon barrage, no black-out, no enemy bombers to bother us. This is such an obvious advantage that I needn't dwell on it. And yet I don't think that this will seem the most important thing about our Canadian training when the war is over. What will count then is the opportunity we had of seeing a new world, a different way of life, and, above all, another people. It was a unique opportunity.

You see, we were not only flying over this new world, we were living in it. It was like studying Canada first through a telescope then through a microscope. During those 300-mile flights over Ontario and the Great Lakes, and later a 1,000 miles east, over New Brunswick, we seemed to absorb the essence of a whole countryside in the passing of an afternoon. Vast panoramas impressed themselves on our minds. Sometimes, as in northern Ontario, the picture was that of a giant jigsaw puzzle of brown and green and silver; of endless forest and bush broken up by fantastically shaped lakes; a land where there are few men, but moose and deer and wolves in plenty; a country of strange wild names – Muskska, Omenee, Nottiwasaga Lake, Shawinigan Falls.

On other days our navigation flights would take us over the vast geometrical pattern of Canadian farmland that lies farther south. Quite a different picture here. No longer a jigsaw puzzle, but a chessboard whose giant squares are divided by dead-straight roads streaking across the country for mile upon mile. And for chessmen there are the cylindrical silos that stand like sentinels by every barn and farmyard; sometimes you can look down into their hollow depths as you pass overhead.

In these parts the place names are no longer wild and romantic: they are old friends from Britain and Europe, mixed up in the oddest confusion. You may go northward from London and arrive at Southampton; southward, and reach Glencoe. You can fly from Moscow at 10 o'clock, and be at either Bannockburn or Sydenham before a quarter past.

As our course proceeded, and we went from one station to another, the panorama in our minds became bigger still, until it included the hills and valleys of Quebec, covered with a million maple trees, and the lonely snow-covered peaks of New Brunswick.

That was the telescopic view. The microscopic view of Canada is the view which you get, not in the air, but on the ground, during your six months' stay. You see, the Commonwealth Air Training Plan will probably take you not to Toronto or Montreal or Quebec, the big cities which every tourist sees, but to some remote training school in the heart of the country. You may find yourself, for example, at a school where the village is seven miles away, and where the nearest town is eighteen miles off, and even then has only 6,000 inhabitants. But you'll get to know this town, as we did. And you will probably learn as much about the essential atmosphere of Canada in one such visit as in five visits to a great cosmopolitan centre like Toronto.

Take the ancient little bus one winter evening over those eighteen miles of country road. You will know when you are getting near the town from the signpost, which in large letters directs you 'Downtown.'

Go downtown. Take a walk round the snowy tree-lined streets of white-painted timber houses, neat, prosperous, well kept, with their long front gardens unhedged and open to the road. Then go into one of the local cafés, sit down in one of the typical horse-box seats, and order your toasted western sandwich, your Hamburger steak, or your pumpkin pie. Someone has put a nickel in the slot of the Wurlitzer phonograph, an elephantine monstrosity of red, green, and yellow glass lit up from within, and the whole air begins to quake with hoarse, booming music. How well you will get to know the repertoire, or at least those bits of it which the town likes – 'Amapola,' 'Chattanooga Choochoo,' and 'Why don't we do this more often?'

In a little while a crowd of fellows and girls stroll in, noisy and jolly after an evening's skating, dressed in brightly coloured woollen caps, scarves, and wind breakers. This is Canada! Outside it has begun to snow. But the ancient little bus turns up at midnight, ready to plough its way back to the airfield. Half-way home, the drifts become deep. The bus begins to skid; roars ineffectively; stops. You and twenty-five other airmen tumble out, and in the midst of a driving blizzard dig the bus out of three feet of snow. The glare of the headlamps, like a spotlight on the stage, makes a dramatic little incident of the straining, struggling group, with their collars turned up and greatcoats blowing in the gale. More lights, but these in the distance. They belong to the snow plough, creeping slowly along towards you behind a mist of churned-up snow. Eventually a path will be cleared, and the bus will be able to go on its way.

Yes, this is Canada! But the Commonwealth Air Training Plan did more than show us Canada and the Canadian way of life. It introduced us to the Canadians themselves, with whom we flew in the same planes, worked in the same classrooms and lived in the same barracks. And you can't do that without each coming to know the other a good deal better.

On our side we liked their tremendous liveliness, their sense of fun, above all their sociability. They don't suffer from the English tendency to regard every unidentified stranger as a suspect, if not an enemy. To the Canadians you are a friend unless and until you show them in some way that you don't want to be. Another characteristic which we experienced at first hand was their natural directness and openness: they don't believe in hiding their real thoughts under a poker face. They dislike anything that smacks of pretentiousness, snobbery, or insincerity; for all of these they have a good old army word.

This friendly and sociable spirit did a lot to make us Englishmen feel at home out there, for it wasn't confined to the Canadian boys on our course. There was 'Aunt Lil' of the little wooden snack-bar in the village, who asked two of us to share Christmas dinner with the family. There was Mrs. Kendrie of Hamilton, who, seeing us at the next table in a hotel when she happened to be dining, quietly paid for our dinners, sent us some cigarettes, and slipped away before we could thank her. There were those countless friends who gave us long rides in their vans, lorries, and private cars.

If we learned something about the Canadians, I think they also learned something about us. And at any rate we were able to laugh at our differences. They laughed at the Englishman's 'Cheerio, old boy,' and we could give a pretty good imitation of the noisy Canadian greetings that rang down the barracks – 'Hey, Shorty!' 'Hullo there, Slim!' The Canadians swore we couldn't talk English, and in reply one of our party started a school of elocution for Canadians about to visit Britain. 'No, no!' we would hear him saying. 'Not a "part of hart carffee"! Repeat after me – "A pot of hot coffee"!'

Do these things seem trivial? I don't really think they are, for while you can laugh together at your smaller differences, the differences that matter will not arise. And that may be a very important thing in the post-war world.

VII
BOMBS AWAY!

'Only to fly through cloud, through storm, through night
Unerring, and to keep their purpose bright,
Nor turn until, their dreadful duty done,
Westward they climb to race the awakened sun.'
Anon

1. TWELVE LANCASTERS WENT FOR AUGSBURG

You'll want to hear something about the daylight raid on Augsburg that they gave me this V.C. for. The whole idea of the raid was surprise. That was why we simply flew straight at our objective, at under a hundred feet from the ground. In the case of the six Lancasters from the other squadron, surprise was completely achieved. Not one of them was attacked by fighters either on the way out or on the way back, though two were shot down over the target. But, very likely by sheer bad luck, the six Lancasters which I was leading ran into a patrol of 30 or so Jerry fighters six minutes after we had crossed the French coast. And it was then that four out of the six of us were shot down. I believe that we owe our survival to the fact that I took my aircraft down to no more than 25 feet above ground, and my remaining companion followed me.

I wonder if you can imagine what it means for two of these huge four-engined machines to travel across Europe at that height? Of course we had to go up over every line of trees, to follow the contours of the ground, lifting over the hills, coming down in the valleys. Believe me, it's quite a strain to pilot a 30-ton Lancaster, fully loaded, hour after hour, doing that. But I think it was that that saved us. The fighters were going for us from directly behind. I had just seen the painful sight of the aircraft a few feet away to my left crash in flames. We flew with our wingtips almost touching for mutual protection. We saw the red roofs and white houses of a typical French village loom up in front of us. I couldn't see it from my position in the pilot's seat; but my bomb aimer, in the nose of the machine, told me that he could see the barrage of cannon shells from the German fighters, which had missed us, crashing into the roofs of the houses. The French village seemed to him to be going up in flames. Just think what it must have been like for its inhabitants, as the two vast black bombers, their 12 rear machine-guns firing all out, with a horde of fighters after them, spitting cannon shells, swept over them at roof-top height.

I couldn't help thinking it was a bit of a lesson as to what happens to countries which get knocked out and have the war fought all over them.

Well, as you know, eight out of the twelve of us got to the target, and though three were shot down by the ground fire over it, all eight of us bombed it from roof-top height. I know that I for one had to pull up to clear the roof of that main assembly shed where they made the submarine engines.

There I saw the last of my six companions go down; his Lancaster was hit as he ran up, but though it was blazing he went straight on and planted his bombs on the sheds. The photographs taken since show that no submarine engines will come out of those sheds for a very long time.

Thank goodness, I saw him make a perfect forced landing in a field, and firmly believe that he and his crew are prisoners of war.

We suffered heavy losses and I lost good friends in that raid. But we got the target. And that is the main thing. I try not to think about my friends, but about the sailors who will be saved from the torpedoes of those submarines, and the men, women, and children who will eat the food that the ships which would have been sunk, but for our bombs, will now bring safely to them. I know that this is what my friends who went down would like us to think of.

2. A FRESHMAN OVER GENOA

By the rather gloomy points of red lights in the interior of a Stirling I wrote down a rough log of impressions during my first night raid. The distance we travelled was about 1,500 miles, so there was plenty of time to arrange one's thoughts. The crew did much to help the freshman among them taking notes. The most irrelevant ideas kept intruding, and over the Alps I remember wondering whether my Scots terrier puppy would have recovered from her hiccups yet. Here is the log:

5 p.m. Just before the Stirling door is slammed, a ginger-haired member of the ground crew bending down drops a pack of cards from his top pocket. His eye catches mine as I tie a knot in myself trying to buckle on the parachute harness. 'We're having a game of solo to-night,' said he. 'Good luck,' say I. 'Good luck,' says he, and bangs the door.

5.11. Airborne, and I didn't know it. I looked out of the astro-dome to see the take-off, and discovered we were about 500 feet up – so smooth had been the getaway. Several other Stirlings circled around to gain height and prepared to set course. I can see a searchlight crew below fussing around and polishing up.

6.5. We crossed the coast. It's still light enough to observe that the white line of sea breakers, because of the state of the tide, makes the map look silly.

A fine sunset as we fly over the Channel. I go down to the bomb-aimer's hatch to spot the moment when we cross the coast of France. But dark blue imperceptibly changes to dark cloud and I can smell the mist in the aircraft. So the only news I get that we are over the enemy territory is the gentle evasive action. No flak.

6.50. We are passing through a rainstorm.

7.30. St. Elmo's fire round the airscrews. I can see circles of flame shimmering round the propellers, and the front gunner reports blue darts on his gun barrels and flame trickling round the metal of the turret. This lasts about ten minutes.

We are climbing for the Alps. The F/Engineer switches on oxygen. The atmosphere of tenseness and efficiency takes one back to a hospital operating theatre. The smell and feel of the oxygen apparatus on my face are strange and like an anaesthetist's mask.

8.14. I am lying flat over the bottom blister and can see a lake where before the war we had some good trout fishing.

The foothills of the Alps come into view – black, massive surfaces checkered with purplish white, growing whiter as we climb.

The captain suggests that if I come forward again I shall soon see Genoa. Clumsily I clamber ahead, my dangling intercom. winding around the F/Engineer's neck. In his baleful red light he looks up, grins, and shouts, 'How are you feeling?' 'Fine,' I say. 'Liar,' said he. 'Don't worry. We all go through it on our first trip.'

Trying to joke, I have to stop half-way for lack of breath and plug in again for oxygen.

'Over there,' says the captain. 'Genoa.' No future being in Genoa on a night like this.

There is no cloud and faintly we can see the Bay and the Mediterranean. We are the first aircraft on, and suddenly I realise that that cluster of searchlights and mass of white gun flashes is what we have to go through.

We are nearer, and red fire balls are ascending.

9.5. We start violent jinking. I can see the glow of our exhausts, and imagine that all Genoa is watching them. As we weave, I see the hump of the outer engines rising and falling against the vivid light of flashes, flak, and searchlights. I hang tight to the edges of the astro-dome.

9.13. 'Open bomb doors,' comes through the intercom., and then, 'O.K., bomb doors open.'

I lift my oxygen mask and bite into a small English Newton apple. For some reason it gives me great pleasure to munch a Newton apple over Genoa on Saturday night.

Searchlights roam across the propellers, edge the wing tips, flick the tail, and, fantastic as it seems, never catch us.

Gun flashes below reveal the blocks of buildings, and the red fire balls come nearer on both sides when the captain levels out for the bombing run.

9.16. Bombs gone. Now the jinking begins again. As we thread between the beams I count 27 searchlights below.

Down below I can see a row of incendiaries – the first fires in Genoa to-night. Proudly the rear gunner observes to me that these are golden and broad, which means that they have turned into real fires. Incendiaries, on their own, he says are silver-glittering and sharp.

9.30. Flares illuminate the bay, and Genoa is floodlit. Jets of flak spew up towards us. Within ten minutes of the first flares the port is burning. Bomb flash adds to bomb flash, and the last searchlight is dowsed. Only the town is alight.

Soon, it seems, I am peering again at the Alps lit by searchlight, and slowly the scene merges into clouds over the plains of France. Static electricity and lightning once more bring a kind of dangerous beauty to the Stirling and then hail beats on the windows. The flak at Genoa, the captain tells me, as we side-track the flak of Northern France, was mild and a proper initiation for the novice.

01.36. The friendly lights of our flare-path back at base. 'Eight and a half hours,' says the navigator. '1,500 miles.' The searchlight which I saw being polished up before flicks on for a moment and extinguishes.

' O.K., V for Victor,' says base. 'You can land now.' Ginger from the ground crew comes in and asks how I got on. 'Weren't you scared?' said he. 'Bombs right on Genoa,' I say, and ignore the question. 'And you?' I ask. 'Cor,' says he, 'I won 2s. 3d.'

So to the interrogation room where the captain wisecracks. And then to the operational breakfast with bacon and egg and hot tea. And the 'line book' already waiting on the table. I mentioned quite truthfully that at first I thought our incendiaries were Italian searchlights, and that remark, of course, goes straight into the 'line book,' but I am forgiven, being a novice. I go home and am thankful to find that the puppy has indeed got over her hiccups. She is asleep but faintly wags her tail.

3. V FOR VIC

Let me tell you a true story about a Wellington bomber called 'V for Victory,' one of a squadron engaged on a recent operation over Germany. All the other aircraft were back, but V for Vic was well over its E.T.R. or Estimated Time for Return. Signals were listening out, the Intelligence and Ops. Staff on the *qui vive*. Suddenly they heard its call sign. In she came, touched down safely, and the ground crew who had been waiting so anxiously for her clustered round and waited for the crew to climb out. But the only man to leave the aircraft was the pilot, a Squadron Leader with the D.S.O. and D.F.C. The places of his crew were empty. Somehow he had brought his aircraft home alone.

He told his story. Soon after reaching his target, he had been engaged by the guns of the enemy. There was flak all around, some of it uncomfortably close, but even when his wireless operator told him over the intercom. that sparks were coming through the floor of the aircraft he did not worry unduly. A pilot of his experience would know that his crew could handle a bit of a fire with the extinguishers. He carried on. What he could not know was that one of the flares carried in the aircraft had been set alight. Soon the sparks were flames, and a moment later the whole Wellington lit up and he was suddenly blinded. The smoke and fumes were choking them, and the pilot could see nothing but a vivid yellow glare – worse than trying to look into a blinding flash. Then he thought it was all up with them. Their aircraft had become a blazing target in the sky. Even if it wasn't hit, it would probably soon break up.

Thinking they only had a few seconds to bale out, he gave the order. He saw his crew go down, the rear gunner, the bomb aimer, the navigator, then the wireless operator, all with their parachutes. It was his turn last. He left his pilot's seat and groped for his 'chute. He searched everywhere, but he couldn't find it. There was only one thing left for him to do. To try and crash-land the machine. For some reason the German gunners left it alone, perhaps because they considered the plane, now like a flaming torch in the sky, completely finished. As he dived down, he weaved the aircraft about to try and put out some of the flames, so that, as he neared the ground, he might have more time to look for a place to land. As he side-slipped his eyes became more used to the glare and suddenly, while he was still at flying height, the flames went out. It was as dark as it had been light.

The plane flew on. He tried to pull himself together, but for a while it was all he could do to keep the aircraft level. Then he remembered the last course his navigator had set for him for their return journey to England, and he decided to take the longest chance of his life – to fly a huge bomber which normally takes five men, all doing an essential job. He decided to tackle them all single-handed. He was still over enemy territory, there was still more flak to be gone through, still more searchlights to be evaded, and worst of all he might meet enemy fighters. What then, since he had no one to man his guns? He set his course for Dieppe, because he believed that if he could get that far he could get the rest of the way home. He made Dieppe, recognised it, and started out to fly across the Channel.

But one disaster was yet to befall him. Over the sea both his engines stopped. Then, if it had not been for that wonderful contrivance called the 'automatic pilot,' or more familiarly by air crews just 'George,' he would have been lost. When 'George' is plugged in, an aircraft will fly itself in fair weather with only a slight hand adjustment from time to time, and since his petrol clock told him the reason for the engines' cut, he had to leave the controls for a few moments and scramble back in the aircraft to turn on the emergency petrol supply. He managed it; but before he could get back into his seat, on came one of the engines with a roar. This sent the aircraft down in a spiral dive; which even the miraculous 'George' could not prevent, since it takes a live pilot to fly a bomber on one engine.

Down they went from 4,000 feet towards the sea, and they were not far from it when the Squadron Leader got back to his seat. But he did get there in time to straighten the aircraft and start up the other engine.

And so he lived to bring his aircraft home and to tell the story.

4. ENEMY FIGHTER DEAD ASTERN

The job of a gunner is to protect the bomber from fighter attacks. Some gunners go through ops. and never see a fighter. One of the chaps in my squadron shot one down on his very last operation. It was the only one he had ever seen. Things have worked out differently for me. I have taken part in 21 ops., and seen fighters on almost every trip, and sometimes had encounters with them. In fact, we had nine fighter attacks on our first five trips.

Good evasive action is essential if a bomber is to get the best of a fighter, and good evasive action depends on the gunner's judgment and the pilot's co-operation. The gunner tells his skipper just when to turn in order to spoil the fighter's aim.

On my first war flight – to the docks at Le Havre – a fighter came at us. Being inexperienced, I gave the order to turn a fraction too soon, and he almost got us. The skipper's violent turn upset me almost as much as the Jerry, and my first burst missed. I managed to hit him with the next two, and that was enough for him.

A gunner and his captain have to work closely together, and my pilot is a marvel when there are fighters about. Many times he has shaken them off by a single turning movement, without a shot being fired. He gave me a grand chance to shoot down a Ju. 88 when returning from Bremen. The fighter attacked several times from port and starboard, and though we avoided his fire he managed to get right underneath our tail.

Despite violent turns he stayed there for four minutes, which seemed like half an hour. I was standing up, operating my turret, and only getting an occasional glimpse of him. He fell back a little, but I held my fire and asked the skipper to pull the nose up. How he ever managed it I don't know, but I shall never forget the way that giant machine seemed to shudder and hang on its propellers as my bullets smashed through the Hun. There was a red glow and two white ones from each engine, as he caught fire and rolled over. As the Halifax fell out of this manoeuvre, I was thrown back and lost sight of the enemy, but I heard the mid-upper gunner shout, 'You've got him!' When I next saw him he was a mass of flames.

That is a good example of how a tail gunner and his skipper must work together. It is not a one-man show when a Junkers, Messerschmitt, or Focke-Wulf is shot down. It is often the work of at least four members of the crew – the tail gunner, the mid-upper gunner, the pilot, and the engineer who keeps a look-out through the astro-dome.

On our way to Karlsruhe one night, we had just avoided an attack by a pair of Me. 109s when we were forced into action by an F.W. 190. It made four very determined passes at us, and each time we swished out of his way. Each time he pulled out for another go, you could almost hear the German pilot thinking, 'Where have they gone now?' We really foxed him. After his fourth attempt he followed us for several minutes, then waggled his wings in what seemed to me to be a salute, and sheered off. I would like to meet that chap after the war.

5. SIXTY-FIVE DEGREES OF FROST

Cold may not sound to you to be one of the worst dangers which a bomber crew has to face; but in some ways it is. It's cold on a different scale from anything you experience on the ground; cold that bites at you, that attacks your will power, that makes you physically and mentally incapable of doing anything.

Naturally our bombers have heating systems. Hot air from the engine is blown on to you down a sort of thing that looks like a speaking-tube. But the other night, no sooner had we taken off than we found that our heating system had packed up. There was nothing else wrong with the aircraft. Peter – that's our pilot – didn't say anything about going back. So we set course and carried on. But it meant six hours of cold that would take a bit of living through.

These Hampdens are grand aircraft: but they are a bit cold at times, and the coldest place in them happens to be where the rear gunner – that's me – has to sit. I'm in a sort of bulge which looks like a coal scuttle – we call it the tin – which sticks out from the bottom of the aircraft, at the back under the tail.

The flight out to Emden was quite uneventful; just cold; and then getting colder and colder as we gained height. It was a lovely clear night, and we soon found our target – our navigator doesn't make mistakes. There was about the usual amount of flak, but it didn't worry us. As a matter of fact that was a bad sign.

It was the cold; there was about 65 degrees of frost up there over Emden. That amount of cold begins to make you indifferent. You feel the pain of it, but in a way you don't even mind that much. We did a nice run up, our navigator got his sights on, and down went our bombs. I had to look out for the flashes – I saw them too – and also to throw out my incendiaries. I always take a few extra incendiaries with me in my scuttle, even when we have a full load of H.E. bombs, just for luck. The back of the tin was made of this perspex stuff, and it opens rather like a sash window except it's on the curve. You have to pull out a catch and then push the perspex window up.

Well, I got it open all right. That brought a blast of air at 65 degrees of frost in at me. Then I had to fuse my incendiaries. It's rather a niggling little job – pulling out a pin and getting your fingers into a little wire loop. My big outside gloves had to come off, of course. But I pulled the thin ones off too, to try and get the job done quickly. This was a mistake. The moment my fingers touched the metal they went dead and powerless. It's a nasty sensation. I couldn't even begin to fuse those bombs. Then I realised I couldn't possibly work my guns either. I guessed the wireless operator was in the same boat, and he was, too. So I knew that if a night fighter came for us we were helpless.

There was nothing to be done about it, though. So I tried to get my gloves on again, but I found I couldn't. I must say I thought that meant that my hands would be gone. Then I realised that the perspex was still open: that was why I was freezing up so quickly. I began to fumble with the catch to get it shut. For a long time I couldn't get any kind of a grip on it. Then I knelt on my guns to get more purchase. The movement must have stirred me up enough to realise that if I didn't get the perspex shut I was done for; no one could stand for hours with it open.

I got one of my bent fingers round the catch, and it came out. Now the curved perspex should push down shut. I heaved at it. It stuck. I heaved again. It was frozen fast. But the exertion was waking me up. I went on fighting it. You know how maddening it is when some gadget won't work. My life may have depended on my making this one work. I just went on heaving; then I tried to jerk it. Nothing happened. I couldn't think of anything else to do. I just went on at it. Then suddenly it shut. I had been fighting it for twenty minutes. After that it wasn't so bad. I still couldn't get my gloves on. But I worked my hands back into my sleeves, and that saved them. Then Peter brought us down lower and lower so that it got less cold. We'd found the target and bombed it, and we all got back none the worse.

6. 'I'D NEVER BEEN TO PARIS BEFORE'

I'd never been to Paris before, but it looked exactly as I imagined it would look: we'd studied a lot of guide books and photographs before we set out.

We flew very low all the way across to avoid attack, and we saw masses of horses in the fields. The Beaufighter is pretty quiet, and we didn't seem to disturb the horses and cattle very much, but we took some photographs of them. Some horses were rearing up as we came over the fields, and one of them was a white horse and you can almost see the whites of his eyes in our picture. We could see the Eiffel Tower when we were 30 to 40 miles from Paris, which helped out with the navigation, because we were much too low to have a look at Paris from above. But it was a very nice day – plenty of sun, and we could see quite easily where we were going. We took a bearing from the Eiffel Tower and came in smack over the Defence Monument, and then headed straight for the Arc de Triomphe. I said to Sergeant George Fern, my observer, 'Are you ready with the first flag?' and he said, 'Yes, I'm ready all right, but the slipstream is nearly breaking my arm.' He was pushing this furled flag down a flare shoot into the slipstream from the propellers, and at the right moment he let her go.

We'd experimented quite a bit with the flags before we started, and they were both weighted and folded so that they'd stream as soon as they were released. However, we couldn't stop to see exactly where the first dropped; but I'm glad to see that Vichy says it fell right on the tomb of the Unknown Warrior, which is, of course, just where you'd want it to be.

One of the things we wanted to look at particularly was the Ministry of Marine, because it was crammed with Huns, and we had something for them too. We spotted that quite easily, and turned north towards the Opera, and then out again. On this first circuit the people in the street didn't seem to pay a great deal of attention to us. Of course there was a certain amount of traffic in the street, which may have covered up the noise of our engines, but there wasn't anything like the traffic there is in London, and we didn't see any motor buses in the Champs Elysées.

We didn't go very far before we turned for our second circuit, and this time we came in as low as we dared in case they had any light ack-ack on the roof-tops. Actually I was too busy watching out for chimney pots and steeples to notice any ack-ack fire at all; Fern warned me that some tracer did actually pass close by us, but certainly the aircraft was never hit at all. On this second circuit we didn't make quite the same tour. We turned south a bit towards the river so we could come square up to the Ministry of Marine, and when we were right in line at a range of about 500 yards we let fly with our four cannon, and I saw the sparks flying off the building. We hadn't any time to see whether the shells burst inside, but a good many went through the windows. We sprayed the place from base to apex, and only cleared the roof with the aircraft about 5 feet. While I was doing this, my observer was shouting encouragement and pushing out the second flag, which we hoped would fall slap across the front door.

There was much more interest taken in this circuit of ours, and people were running about the streets to have a good look at us, and we noticed one or two faces at the window actually peering down at us. We saw a number of German military cars stopped in the street with the Huns standing round them, and others of them were dodging round the trees in the Avenue, but we couldn't let fly at them because there were too many civilians about. Some of the civilians were waving to us. Fern says he saw some German soldiers trying to take cover behind a lorry. One of them was very fat, and he was shaking his fist at us.

I'm sorry I can't tell you any more about our visit to Paris – it was very short, only five or six minutes – but I'd like to go again with all the photographs we took, and see how it looks with both feet on the ground.

7. THE RED INSIDE THE WHITE

The other afternoon I flew with a squadron of Bostons on a daylight attack on the docks at Cherbourg. I kept a rough log of my impressions. Here are some of them:

2.25 p.m. The ground crew tuck us in, and in the noise of the engines can do no more than wish us luck by the traditional thumbs-up sign. It makes me feel good.

2.30 p.m. We take off in formation. From my perch in the gunner's dome I can see all the other Bostons racing along the ground. The sense of speed is immense, and I am pushed hard against the tail of the dome.

2.40 p.m. Hedge-hopping south. I am getting some astonishing noises through the intercom. I suppose the crew can understand what they're saying, but it sounds like jabberwocky language to me. I can hear Sugar, the Canadian pilot, laughing.

3 p.m. Bumpy weather. It seems very hot in here. Is it nervousness, air-sickness, or just plain heat? We are doing a good 250 miles an hour, and I shouldn't have thought it could be hot at that speed.

3.15 p.m. It is air-sickness. Blast! But remember, I say to myself, that a Wing Commander, D.F.C., told you he is always air-sick when he's not flying the plane himself. Johnny, the air-gunner, looks at me. I grin wanly. Johnny holds up a piece of chewing-gum and asks through the intercom. if I'd like some. The jabberwocky becomes intelligible. Sugar butts in and, trying to be English, says, 'Thanks awfully. I don't mind if I do.' Johnny, trying to be Canadian, says, 'Gee, Sugar, why don't you fly yer derned Bawston like I taught you?' I take the chewing-gum and feel better.

3.28 p.m. The fighters are joining us in wings. Very comforting sight. I can see a foursome playing tennis down there. 'Oh, good shot, Mary.' I wonder what the score will be when we get back. It's a glorious afternoon for it. Heigh-ho for the days of iced fresh lemonade.

3.38 p.m. There go the white cliffs of somewhere or other. Hope to see you again soon, white cliffs.

3.50 p.m. Quite suddenly it is intensely cold. I am not wearing gloves and my left hand is numb. I am in the under-gunner's position now, looking out over a large hole. We have climbed to 12,000 feet. The sea looks completely stiff. I can see the waves clearly but they are motionless, like a solid mass of uneven grease.

3.55 p.m. French coast on the horizon. Physically this is exhilarating, and I keep saying to myself, 'Well, you're not scared – yet.'

4 p.m. We cross the coast. Here comes the flak. The white flak bursts are higher and nearer and more frequent. Goldy, the observer, calls out, 'Don't worry, Leslie, until you can see the red inside the white.'

4.3 p.m. I can see the red inside the white, but quite honestly I am not worried. The whole thing seems too efficient to worry. I feel for the handle of the parachute and touch the dinghy.

4.4 p.m. Bomb doors open on every Boston in the formation.

4.5 p.m. Bombs gone. In my excitement I put my head as far out of the hole as I can reach and watch them going down, down, down. The first bursts are in the dock water, but then I see the direction for which the stick is heading. White mushrooms of smoke suddenly spout on the dock side. Good.

4.6 p.m. Flak is now very intense. Black puffs as well as white. Violent evasive action. I can see Hun fighters coming up. But I have a wonderful impression of immunity. A sort of godlike feeling that nothing can touch us. I should know better than this.

4.7 p.m. Hell! There goes a Boston. Quite slowly, but he's going down into the sea in a controlled dive. Johnny tells me who the pilot is. I know him. He pulled my leg about the raid in the briefing room and wished me luck. Well, good luck to him now. The Spitfires are fussing about us more than ever. Some of them seem to be flying sideways and others belly first.

4.20 p.m. No sign of England yet. I wonder how long before we're out of the Hun fighter zone. Morse comes cracking in the earphones, and Sugar sings, 'I walked beside ye,' flat in three keys.

4.29 p.m. England. Down a bit and it's warmer. I never felt better, I suppose it's the extra oxygen. Yes, the girls are still playing tennis.

4.50 p.m. We're landing. I say, 'Thank you, Sugar,' and Sugar replies, 'No trouble at all.'

We got back to base. I phoned through to headquarters to give them my usual report. You know the way it goes, 'Bostons of Bomber Command with fighter escort to-day attacked the docks at Cherbourg.' But from now on, every time I write or read that kind of thing, it will touch me a little more deeply, and I shall hold in a little more awe the men who do that job, day in day out, and sing on the way back.

8. OVER THE SNOWLINE AND HOME

We crossed the snowline of the Alps on Saturday night at about ten o'clock. Rocky black became white, mist covered the foothills. We flew up between the high peaks and there, a few minutes later, was Turin. The mid-upper gunner said that from the distance it seemed that the town was already alight. But it wasn't. The blood-red glow came instead from the half-moon rising ahead of us.

The Stirling was at 5,000 feet when the first flare went down over Turin, and a moment or two later there were over 200 flares burning in the sky, each bright enough to light up Turin. As we corkscrewed our way down, dodging between them, I could see the lights glinting on the two long railways and on the river Po, coldly silver and winding. Our pilot stayed at 1,000 feet as we searched for our target. Occasionally we caught the blast from someone else's bursts, and were able to compare the explosion of the big 'teasers' – the 8,000-lb. bombs – with that of smaller bombs. At one moment straight ahead of us a block appeared to boil up and settle down again in flames. We were over the target for half an hour and had time to take stock. Along one street factory buildings on either side were burning, and we could see their reflections in the bitumen road. In another part, burning blocks were mirrored in the windows opposite.

Flak occasionally came near – green, red, and yellow, pretty as a Christmas tree but far less useful. We lurched once and thought they had hit us. But on landing we found a dent in the tail-plane; it had been caused by a flare casing falling on us from above. It had sheared off some rivets.

All this time we were looking for our target. Time and again I pointed out tempting-looking factories, but the pilot took no notice of me. Then we found the factory we were after and peered at it in the now rather smoky light. The captain hummed and ha-ed, while we looked at it from every angle. Our bomb aimer, who is a deer stalker back in New Zealand, has got keen eyes, and he identified the factory. Then the captain said, 'O.K.,' and we bombed the factory with a quick stick. We saw six of our bombs fall across the factory. They started something up all right.

A Stirling pilot who bombed another factory that night said that after bombing it looked as though a small boy had drawn his hand across a straight pattern in the sand and spoilt the design. Our factory – pardon the tone of proprietorship – looked to me as though the same boy had been at work in a different way. It appeared as though a shower of stones had been thrown into a pool. As the water spreads out and then strongly plops up in the centre, so was the bombed part of the factory. Smoke flattened out in ripples, and then in the centre the high flames rose up. Soon the red flames were chequered with green.

We climbed up and had another peep. Our fires had attracted other bombs. When we left, there was a glow there about half a mile in diameter, and the green colours kept darting over the red. Our gunners sent a stream of tracer bullets into a flak position, silencing the gun. Then we flew back across the peaks, over the snowline and home, with the moon coming up to light the way.

WINGS ACROSS AFRICA

'Fly to the desert, fly with me.'
Thomas Moore

1. 'THE DESERT IS A FUNNY PLACE'

I've been 14 months in the desert, and when I left it was almost like leaving a family – I was leaving so many chaps that I knew and was friendly with. Because of the conditions out there, you do get to know everybody, and there's an extraordinarily good feeling amongst everybody. That is one of the compensations of life out there. There aren't many. Most of the time you never get away from aircraft. All day long you've people talking about aeroplanes, and tactics, and serviceability, and so on, and at night-time there's no other topic of conversation except flying.

Yes, it's a seven-days-a-week job for months on end, and there's nowhere to get away to. Alexandria is the nearest city – you get a couple of days there every two or three months. Everybody, of course, lives in tents. The day starts half an hour before dawn. The engines are warmed up and uncovered. Breakfast is somewhere around 7 o'clock or 7.30 for the airmen, who line up with their plates, and it's dished out to them – some sort of porridge, not too good because it's made with water that's well chlorinated and usually brackish, and tea made with the same stuff, which although you get used to it is hardly drinkable. Lunch is the same sort of thing – a slice of bully-beef with hard biscuit, and you can have margarine, and of course, more 'chi' again – that's Arabic for tea. You all get a gallon of water per day, from the C.O. to the lowest A.C.H.; half of that goes to the cookhouse and the other half gallon is used for washing, shaving, and so on. You shave every second or third day, and then there's cleaning teeth and washing. So if you want a bath you've got to save up – and that takes you a week probably. But then everybody smells the same, so it doesn't matter. It cancels out. And even bully-beef – it's wonderful what you can do with bully-beef when you try. You can have bully-beef with sand, without sand (sometimes), fried, stewed, curried, hot or cold – quite a variation. And then there's the grand day when they get a load of eggs up. You can have them hard-boiled, or soft-boiled, fried, or poached. You can do a lot with eggs.

The desert is a funny place: it gets a hold on you. During the heat of the day it's just barren and featureless, absolutely miles and miles of nothing – just little patches of shrubs about knee-high. But in the dawn and at sunset the lighting effects are amazing. In the evening, just after the sun finally disappears, a wonderful green light shows all round the western horizon. It lasts for about two minutes, while all the brilliant colours given off by the dust in the atmosphere, gold and brown and purple and so on, come out vividly and then fade away. And then the green light fades away, and the stars come out. I've never seen that green light anywhere else. You don't get it in the Sahara or the Gobi Desert. Apparently it's unique to the Western Desert. You get the same sort of thing at dawn. There's a gold and red glow, and all of a sudden the sun jumps up above the horizon. If you're flying over the Mediterranean at dawn, the sea changes in colour as you watch it, from emerald green to azure blue and deep blue. It's really beautiful. And then there's the background of the desert along the coastline, looking so golden and fresh and clean in the dawn. Even the dirty tents below you look clean. But an hour after the sun's up – gosh, it's awful!

But you don't want to hear about fancy sky effects. You want to know what the flying is like. Well, I should say it's like nowhere else on earth. There are no landmarks in the desert, and the heat makes such a haze that there's no horizon at all. You've got nothing to fly on. I've often been up at say 18,000 feet with reasonably good visibility. I could see an aircraft six or seven miles away all right. But below me was just haze. You're sort of waffling through the air, working on your instruments and your general sense of the levelness of your wings. But if you're not careful you can easily be flying with one wing down.

Navigation, of course, is easy if you are anywhere near the coastline, because you know what to look for from the shape of the coast. But when you move inland, as you must necessarily do when you start operations, you have to land on places which are just simply parts of the desert. You search for the darned thing, and land, and while you're doing that you've got to take very great notice of the shade and colour of the ground – dark patches and light patches, and so on. You've got to memorise all that for future use, because one day if you don't find your aerodrome you'll be in a mess. The next one may be 30 or 40 miles away, and you'll be landing the squadron all over the place, and probably write them off with no petrol.

The sandstorms you hear about are usually not sandstorms at all; they're dust storms caused by the churning up of all the transport and tanks, and so on. A sandstorm proper is rather rare. Planes taking off create a miniature sandstorm of their own. From above you can see the sand streaming out behind them for a quarter of a mile. And if he's anywhere near, you bet the enemy can see it too. So we all get into the habit of taking a good look round before we take off. If Jerry is anywhere about, he'll see it and come down quick. Taking off through a dust storm, you're absolutely blind from the time you take off, except that you can see other aircraft 30 or 40 yards away: you've got to fly by your instruments through this brown mass. I've known it go up to 11,000 feet. But then you break through, and you're all right except that you've got no view of the ground at all. You have to fly on your compass to where you're going. On the way back, you've to come down through it to find your aerodrome. If you're near the coastline, you work along it until you see some point that's familiar to you, and then you take a bearing and continue to fly low – ten or twelve feet – until you see tents or something, and hope you recognise them. But you can't afford any mistakes – going at 300 miles an hour, twelve feet above the ground, would be just too bad.

The sand, of course, gets into the engines, everywhere, and the maintenance crews have to work long hours under pretty tough conditions. Every part of the machine, when it's taken out, has to be covered over immediately with a cloth. When the sun goes down, the machines are covered up. There's nothing to do except to go to bed, or yarn and play cards by a kerosene lamp. The only compensations are beer and cigarettes. The beer is bought by the funds of the squadron; no one gets any preference. It's just doled out squarely all round. And yet, despite it all, how these chaps work! They're a grand lot.

The Poles in my squadron were fine – good pilots and desperately keen to kill Germans. That was the one thing they could think of. They didn't think of anything else. Every night they sat there, planning out among themselves more ingenious ways of killing Germans. And after what some of those chaps have been through – well, I can understand it. I remember once a Polish pilot who was flying as Number Two. After his lot had been attacked about four times he was finally shot up and went down in flames. We thought he'd gone and we'd sort of written him off the list. We had lunch, and then about three o'clock in the afternoon an army truck comes up and there he is. Apparently, though on fire, he'd managed to crash-land and then got smartly out of the plane and hopped into a trench in the ground, thinking that they might come down and machine-gun him. So he stayed there till it was all over. When he gets out of the truck he says to us, 'I'm very sorry.' We say, 'Well, *we're* very glad.' He says, 'I'm sorry I was not able to be Number Two. I had to drop away, because I was shot down.' We said, 'Don't worry about that. We're glad to see you back with us.' He said, 'If you take me again as Number Two, I'll not do that again.' Can you beat it?

My own blackest moment happened when I was in a fight about 15 miles out to sea. I got pretty badly shot up, and they put a few slugs in the old hide as well. I went into a spin which lasted 8,000 feet, but I pulled out just above the water; I thought then that I was all right. A good part of my dashboard had gone, the glass had gone, and the wings were pretty badly shot up, and I was feeling a bit sore myself, feeling a bit sick – from fright and one thing and another – but I thought I was pretty safe. I got in across the coast at Sidi Barrani. I thought I could just pop her down near the shore and swim a bit. I didn't think the enemy would bother about me, seeing me dive down, but all of a sudden streams of smoke started to go past me, two 109s were after me – they'd followed me down.

I thought, 'Well, I've bought it this time definitely.' I did what I could, but a bullet hit the wing again, and that didn't help me very much, and I must have been about a quarter of an hour with those blokes chasing me and skidding, and me all the time trying to turn and watch them, and the sweat just dripping out of my helmet with fright and hard work. And then one of them did a silly thing. He got a little bit over-confident, and when I turned once he just turned round and overshot me, and I put a burst into his belly and he went into the sea. The other chap let me go. It was just on dark, and he probably wanted to go home and was out of ammunition.

I had a long way to go home. We had a refuelling party just at that spot, but they hadn't a doctor or facilities, and I had to fly 30 minutes back in the dark, not feeling too good; but I managed to get in all right with the old kite. The other chaps had seen me skimming past them with a lot of smoke going out of the cockpit so they thought I was badly alight, especially as it was pretty gloomy down by the sea, and they were in the sun. They had sent out reports that I was missing, so we had to get moving pretty quickly to stop them. Of course a fighter squadron doctor doesn't get much practice, so he was quite bucked up when I appeared.

No, it never pays to underrate the Hun. I regard the Germans as reasonably tough propositions. I was always a stickler for flight discipline. The boys wanted, if they were new, to go flying all over the sky alone, until they had learnt the dangers of what would happen. The Germans were good at thinking up traps, so I used to have a notice printed up in the place, 'Use your head, then the guns' – just to remind them. For instance, you might see this sort of thing. You might be flying along under the clouds and then perhaps there'd be an open patch, and an enemy plane or two under that open patch. Well, it always seems to me that the right question is, why should they be there? There's always certain to be something up above, and if a couple of ours rush in to get those two on their own, the others come down and get them. No, there's no such thing as a sitter in the air – or at least there is, but you can't tell beforehand.

2. 'A NUMBER OF TYPES RAN OUT OF THE FRONT DOOR'

I've been fighting since pretty well the beginning of the war, over Dunkirk, the Battle of Britain, and so on, and I enjoyed the fighting in Tunisia better than any. You might wonder why. The fighting in Tunisia is more uncomfortable than any I've known. We didn't have nice comfy messes to come back to with hot and cold water laid on. There are no baths in Tunisia as far as I can make out. Some of us lived in tents, and a little four-roomed cottage served as a mess. It rained about twice a week, enough to keep the ground nicely muddy; the ground crews had to do all their stuff in the open; taking off and landing were often highly hazardous; and yet the great difference between that and all the other fighting I've done was that we were on the offensive. In the Battle of Britain we had the feeling that if we lost, we lost the world – there was no margin, it was too serious; here we didn't have to worry about that, we were at liberty to enjoy our fighting.

Our airfield was the most forward base in North Africa, wire runways laid on a plateau 35 miles west of Medjez El Bab, with a ring of mountains about 2,000 feet high all round it. It was absolutely bare country with just a few cactus, and a few isolated clumps of trees and Arab dwellings, but it was fantastically beautiful, and there were the most terrific sunsets and sunrises over the mountain peaks.

Our main job was patrolling the army and escorting bombers. As a sideline we went out in low cloud, popping below it every now and then and shooting up anything we could see. There were plenty of targets, especially when Rommel moved back into Tunisia – gun batteries, troop concentrations, and supply columns. Once the Guards told us that the Germans had their headquarters in a certain house, so we went and shot the roof off it. A number of types ran out of the front door, and we chased them across the fields. That was a good day. Another one occurred one day when we went right to the Tunisian coast and whipped out of cloud to find some lorries going along a road. As soon as they saw us the lorries pulled into the side – indeed, they pulled into the ditch in their hurry – everybody jumped out, and we machine-gunned them as they were running away. There were about 30 men in each lorry, and we hose- piped them as they scrambled over each other, and scrambled them still further.

As I said, we are definitely on top out there; but that doesn't mean to say that there isn't a lot of opposition. You can't have air superiority everywhere all the time; there aren't enough aeroplanes in the world to make sure of that. Our airfield used to get shot up a good deal, and we made sure of having plenty of slit-trenches handy. Driving from the mess to the aircraft we always had a gun sticking out of the roof of the car and a man spotting. We were quite often attacked, and one of the pilots has probably destroyed two Junkers 88's in that way before the real day's work started. In fact, the pilots got so anti-aircraft-minded that they formed their own light ack-ack team, mostly using captured German guns given to us by our friends the paratroops, and as C.O. I had to put up a notice in the mess, 'No tommy-guns should be fired at the breakfast table.'

The Germans have a lot of their best fighters in Tunisia. They use nothing but the Focke-Wulf and the Me. 109G. However, we can more than cope with them. I remember one particular group, the famous Battle-of-Britain Ace of Spades squadron; we quite often came across them, with good results; we shot down one of their best pilots on our own aerodrome, a highly decorated gentleman.

Why is it that our pilots are better than the Germans? Probably the proportion of veterans on both sides is about the same. Quality of aircraft; not much in it. We have airfields usually with wire runways and mud everywhere else; they have well-established aerodromes with concrete runways. Yet our men are definitely on top. What's the reason? The answer is, of course, morale. When you come to think of it, the R.A.F. has never been defeated as the German Air Force has, in Libya, for instance, where they even left their ground-crews and flew away, and Göring sent them a message saying they'd let the side down. Our chaps are on the up-and-up, they're definitely enjoying themselves out there, and nothing can stop them.

3. FORTRESSES OVER TUNISIA

A month or so ago I was talking to two American Air Force colonels in Tunisia. They had both been fighter pilots in France in the last war. Very soon we started swapping theories about fighter tactics; and they were very interested in the way we set about the Huns, from the Battle of Britain onwards. We got so interested in working it all out, that at last they said they wanted to invite me to go and visit their front-line squadrons and talk to their pilots. When they got as far as that, they moved pretty quickly. Almost before I'd had time to tell them to choose somebody else I was whisked off to some very senior officers, and they got in touch with our people, and within 24 hours I found myself in one of their bombers, with an escort, on my way.

I was pretty nervous about it, but I started off with a considerable admiration for the Americans, which makes introductions easier. I'd seen them in action, both over Northern France and over Tunisia.

We covered one of their big daylight Fortress raids over Tunis and Bizerta with our Spitfires; and I'd never seen anything exactly like it before. The flak was of every kind, light and heavy – it reminded me of the flak you get over Ostend or any of the tender coastal regions; and it was very accurate indeed even at the height of the Fortresses. But the Americans sailed straight on over the target and dropped a very heavy weight of bombs with extreme accuracy. When they'd finished, smoke and fires covered the whole area. It's really a terrific sight to see these huge Fortresses sailing along in perfect formation thousands of feet above ground, and dropping bomb after bomb with perfect precision in spite of all the A.A. bursts. On a job like that the fighter escort can dodge to some extent, but once they're on the target the bombers have to hold their course whatever the flak's like, so that they can get a perfect sight, and that's what the Americans did on this trip. There wasn't a sign of wavering in spite of the monstrous flak.

So I did know something about them before I visited their squadrons. But I didn't know the half of it. It really was an eye-opener to be up with them and sometimes to go out with them. One of the best shows they did while I was there they wouldn't let me go on, but I saw the whole picture. One day a reconnaissance discovered on a German airfield about 150 grounded aircraft, mostly Junkers. They showed me the photographs. A lot of these aircraft were tucked away in one corner of the airfield. They sent out an immediate daylight expedition of Fortresses to get those fellows, and they brought back the pictures to show what they'd done towards that laudable object. They seemed to me to have done everything that was necessary. The clutch in the corner was torn to pieces by fragmentation bombs. A perfect piece of work, in my opinion. The stronger the magnifying glass, the more pieces you could see. The rest of the airfield was spattered with bits of aircraft – really lovely.

I spent a lot of time with the fighters too. One day 10 Junkers attacked one of their forward aerodromes. They shot down nine of them within about 15 minutes.

All the Americans I met were tigers. They were so keen on getting the Hun, it was very remarkable indeed. They've got amazing determination and guts. They not only do the bombing and the fighting, they talk about it. They talked about fighting tactics for hours, and told me how they handle our Spits and their own P. 38s, P. 40s, and P. 39s – the Lightnings, Kittyhawks, and Airacobras. I picked up a lot from them, ideas of both theory and practice, and they put me through every possible sort of examination. Any sort of hint or tip that they can use they'll have. If anybody's got a bit more experience than they have, they want it if it'll help to down another Hun. People at home here or on the other side of the Atlantic can be perfectly sure that in the American Air Force in Tunisia there's a very sharp and formidable weapon, and it hurts all right. A few lines in a dull communiqué – but I can tell you it means that something's been lopped off or battered or sunk or blown into small pieces, with the most deliberate care and persistence. So far as the enemy is concerned, the 12th American Air Force and the R.A.F. in those parts are one force.

4. IT'S NEVER TOO LATE TO COME BACK

It is odd, I sometimes think, that one shouldn't know beforehand that things are going to happen. It's at the back of one's mind, of course, that things can go wrong; but when it comes to the point, on any particular occasion, somehow one never thinks they will. So to us it was just another trip that night. Same plane, same crew, same target, same 'cheerio,' and 'see you in the morning.' And we set off.

We made our 800-mile journey as usual, found our target as usual, and were given our usual reception of searchlights and flak. We made our bombing run, navigator told us bombs had gone, and then, actually on his last word, the thing happened. Jerry had caught us well and true. I remember a series of blinding flashes, cracks, and sounds of splintering. The skipper suddenly let go his hold on the control column and wiped his eyes. He couldn't see, and blood was running into his eyes. Meanwhile, our plane was diving at nearly 300 miles per. I remember wondering whether the plane had got a date down there. I scrambled to the front turret and let out the gunner and got back to the cockpit, yanked out our injured skip, took his place at the controls, and pulled the plane out of her dive. I checked over damage, and found port engine useless – smoke and flames pouring out – so cut off juice and feathered prop.

It takes a long time to tell, but it didn't take long to do. It was a nasty sight, that stilled airscrew, all the more because our remaining engine was liable to pack up at any moment. Hadn't enough guts to keep us up for long, that was clear. We were losing height steadily. Speed around 75 to 80. 'Sparks' was sending out our identity and decreasing height. I remember wondering what Base would think when they heard it, and what we should think when we couldn't send any more – if we could think then. We had only a few minutes to go, as it turned out. Crew were patching up skipper and heaving all movable stuff of any weight overboard. Then suddenly, right in front of us, mountains! We missed the scrubs on the top of that first ridge by a few feet. We were right among the hills, and couldn't climb the kite out of them.

I turned up a ravine in the hope of twisting a way out. One felt like a fly. No opening; then – hullo, what's this? Clouds? It wasn't. It was a mountain, dead ahead. That's the end! Sorry, blokes. Only one thing to do now. Don't fly into hillside. Wait until you can see scrubs and pull nose right up. Don't forget petrol. Here it comes! Up! Up! Up! Ugh! Petrol off and then the sickening crash as we hit the hill.

Rear gunner told us afterwards he went out at once, but I didn't. I remember the sound as if every piece of the kite had flown apart. And that wasn't the end. The kite began to slide and roll down the hill, ripping and breaking to pieces as she went. My mouth got full of dirt and scrub. There were whacks and smashes at us inside as rocks tore through the fuselage. I clutched the control column. A final bump – I remember warm blood running down my face, hands and neck ... and then ... out.

Coming to, I heard someone shouting our names. Good, I thought, somebody else out besides myself. As a matter of fact we were all out except the rear gunner: there was no sign of him, or of the tail unit or turret. They had broken off when we hit the hillside. We clambered uphill and found him eventually, half in, half out of his turret, covered in blood and knocked out. But he was alive. We pulled him out, and gave him what first aid we had, and lay down to wait for dawn and enough light to inspect our position.

There are some things I suppose one doesn't forget; personally, I don't think I shall ever forget the sights that dawn uncovered for us that morning. The six of us, ragged and covered with blood, were the only signs of life among the wreckage which was strewn for yards and yards over the hillside. Even the hill wore a scar. Our plane had cut deep into the ground as it careered downhill, and had left a bare path which fetched up where we'd caught on a small clump of trees a few feet short of a sheer 600-foot drop.

We did get something out of the wreck – a compass in a padded box, maps, Irving jackets, torn but still useful, two tins of bully-beef, two packets of biscuits, ration chocolate, some concentrated food tablets, a little first-aid kit, and about a gallon of water left in our battered tank.

We made out we were 40 miles east of Benghazi, in the stretch of mountains which runs east parallel with the coast for about one hundred miles. I call them mountains, though they don't rise more than a thousand feet. They're very rugged and wild and absolutely desolate. In those days the British line stopped somewhere near Sollum, which put us, even as the crow flies, a clear 280 miles inside enemy country. Not that we could travel as the crow flies. We should have had no chance down the main roads along the coast. The only chance we had was to make our way two or three hundred miles south-east into the desert, in the hope of picking up British armoured reconnaissance, which in those days was operating hundreds of miles into enemy country on an arc from inside the southern part of our line.

It seemed a pretty hopeless enterprise. Two or three hundred desert miles, with about four days' rations and a gallon of water, all of us knocked about, and one of us too dazed to move. We discussed giving ourselves up, but rejected it. For one thing, it was conceivable that with a smoke fire we might get ourselves spotted by one of our own reconnaissance planes, who'd report us and send someone out for us. We had no matches, but I had a lighter, which I still have.

When at the end of the first day we heard our planes going over to give Benghazi one more pasting, we made out we had covered something under ten miles, and that was much more than we managed in the next three days. There are two roads through the mountains, joining up with the main coast road through Derna. We crossed the first at night-time. We got to the edge of the second one on the afternoon of the third day. We felt pretty bad then. We were very short of food, and our water was nearly out. We had an idea! Between us, we carried one Very pistol and a small revolver. One of us – I think it was Geoff, he was pretty hefty – was to get up on to the road and stop a lorry. The rest of us were somehow to jump on the crew and knock them out and drive off. That was the idea! It was really a hopeless plan, but we never got a chance to try it. We spent the rest of the daylight in the scrub by the side of the road to see if a lorry or car should come along by itself and give us a chance. But when anything did pass it came by in convoy. Not a single lone truck came along. About 8 p.m. the flow stopped. We waited another hour, and then gave it up, and started off again into the desert.

The details of those days have mixed themselves up a bit, and I can't separate them properly now from one another. One glorious day, I remember, it rained. It may sound strange for a wet day to be glorious, but for us it meant water – water to be had for the catching. We had a large piece of parachute silk with us. We'd been using it for our cut and blistered feet, but now five of us stood in a circle holding out the silk with a stone in the centre to concentrate the drops in one spot. The last of us crouched underneath with a round cigarette tin and the water tank, caught the precious drops, and poured them into the tank.

Our food had given out on the fourth day, and for two or three days we only had one nightly meal, consisting of half a tin of hot water. We heated it up on a bracken fire to help keep us warm. Our weakness got so bad that we could hardly carry the water tank, though it was nearly empty. We strung it to a branch and slung it on the shoulders of two of us, but the pain of the stick bit down into us, and we had to keep changing and stopping to rest.

We also had one small haversack which held our maps and compass. It sounds impossible now, but I remember that haversack bent one's back. You've probably heard a lot of unpleasant things about the desert. Rocks we found were the worst; their windswept edges are as sharp as knives. They cut our boots to pieces. One of us only had a pair of gym shoes to start with. It wasn't good. We all felt pretty bad at times, on the point of giving up. Fortunately, however, one or two of us always felt better than the others. If we'd all felt bad at once, I don't think we should ever have got through. The funny thing was, I don't believe we ever doubted that we should get through O.K. I know it never occurred to me that I should die or anything, and we certainly never talked about dying.

However bad things are, I believe one's always surprised at the time that they're not worse. I remember thinking that about our crash, and that it had really been too easy, and the same too, really, with our trek. We talked about other things. Chips, our wireless operator, had been in the catering trade, and he talked a lot about food. We used to sit down sometimes and thrash things out to keep ourselves steady. But all the same, we wouldn't have got through if it hadn't been for the Arabs.

One evening, when we were feeling pretty bad, we saw a herd of goats on a knoll in the distance. You can guess what that meant. It gave us every kind of hope. We tried to catch up with it before dark, but we couldn't make it. But I think the herder of those goats must have reported us to his tribe, for the next day one of them met us. He asked whether we were 'Engleesi,' but we didn't trust him, and said nothing until he produced evidence in the way of scraps of paper signed by British soldiers. Then out of his satchel he produced six hens' eggs, just one each. We sucked them on the spot. And were they good! We had to wait till the next day when we joined up with his tribe to discover how difficult it was for us to eat solid food again.

Those Arabs certainly were good to us and we shall never forget them. They knew their way about the desert as we would in a park. They hid us under rugs several times when Germans and Italians searched their camp. They looked after us and guided us for ten days. By that time we'd learnt quite a lot, even got to love the sour goats' milk which, the first time we drank it, nearly made us sick. And we learned to eat a juicy bit of sheep like the best of them.

Then one day we spotted the armoured cars: they were our own long-range desert men. We let out a yell and rushed at them. The Arabs were pleased too; we said good-bye to them and thanked them as best we could, and then after a drink and smoke we drove off in style.

We covered 400 miles in the next two days. Those trucks take boulders in their stride. But – I take off my hat to those fellows – by the end of the second day our seats were nearly as bad as our feet. The last part of our journey back to our base camp on the Nile we did by plane. We got a royal reception from our old friends! Our hands were shaken until I thought they would drop off. Free beer for nights and nights, and our story told and re-told.

Now it's over, I'm glad it all happened. People always are, of course. I can only say I am too, and may I add this – if ever you get bored with home, bored with food, and fed up with washing or drinking, have yourself dropped in the desert with no means of support and then get back. Having got back, you'll realise how foolish and extravagant you've been in the past. It might even help the war effort. Some people eat far too much, do themselves too well all round, and don't fully appreciate what they have. I know, I used to be the same at one time. But not now. No, never again.

A bird of the air shall carry the voice,
and that which hath wings shall tell the matter.

Ecclesiastes